TRIBAL
KNOWLEDGE

BUSINESS WISDOM BREWED
FROM THE GROUNDS OF
STARBUCKS
CORPORATE CULTURE

John Moore

KAPLAN) PUBLISHING

RRRSt28.
M784t
2006

This publication is designed to provide accurate and authoritative information in regard to the subject matter covered. It is sold with the understanding that the publisher is not engaged in rendering legal, accounting, or other professional service. If legal advice or other expert assistance is required, the services of a competent professional should be sought.

President, Kaplan Publishing: Roy Lipner
Vice President and Publisher: Maureen McMahon
Acquisitions Editor: Karen Murphy
Development Editor: Trey Thoelcke
Production Editor: Leah Strauss
Typesetter: Todd Bowman
Cover Designer: Jody Billert, Design Literate

Library of Congress Cataloging-in-Publication Data

Moore, John, 1970 May 7-
  Tribal knowledge : business wisdom brewed from the grounds of Starbucks corporate culture / John Moore.
      p. cm.
  Includes bibliographical references.
  ISBN-13: 978-1-4195-2001-3
  ISBN-10:   1-4195-2001-6
  1. Starbucks Coffee Company. 2. Coffee industry—United States. 3. Coffee—United States—Marketing. 4. Corporate culture—United States. 5. Organizational effectiveness—United States. I. Title.
  HD9199.U52S736 2006
  658.8—dc22

                                                          2006018167

Kaplan Publishing books are available at special quantity discounts to use for sales promotions, employee premiums, or educational purposes. Please call our Special Sales Department to order or for more information at 800-621-9621, ext. 4444, e-mail *kaplanpubsales@kaplan.com*, or write to Kaplan Publishing, 30 South Wacker Drive, Suite 2500, Chicago, IL 60606-7481.

Thank you Mom and Dad, for not just being my parents . . . but also being my two best friends.

CONTENTS

DUE. Some Tribal Truths About Delivering Memorable
Customer Experiences

TRE. More Tribal Truths—Creating the Kind of
Workplace You'd Like to Work In

INFINE. Some Parting Truths

What Is Tribal Knowledge?

When Howard Schultz took the reins of Starbucks Coffee in 1987—a mere six stores, along with his own trio of Il Giornale coffee bars—he had the grandiose dream of changing the way Americans drink coffee. Almost 20 years later, Starbucks is by far and away the leader of an industry it created—cozy, welcoming coffeehouses serving specialty coffee and espresso beverages. It is a remarkable story that happened in remarkable ways.

For most Americans who grew up prior to the 1990s, coffee was a necessary, though hardly enjoyable, part of the day. It didn't taste good—that wasn't the point. Just as we do not expect cough syrup to be delicious, most of us didn't demand much from a cup of coffee except a jump start to our mornings, and maybe a jolt of caffeine to pull us out of our post-lunch comas.

Americans had become accustomed to drinking coffee from cheap, inferior robusta coffee beans, scooped out of three-pound tin cans, flavor nuances scorched beyond recognition from cooking on a heated plate for endless hours, and served with powdered creamer to mask its unbearable taste. Then in 1971, Starbucks was founded in Seattle's Pike Place Market by three friends (Jerry Baldwin, Gordon Bowker, and Zev Siegel) who all shared a passion for great-tasting, European-style coffee made from dark-roasted arabica beans. This was coffee that had full flavor without the need of sugar and milk. It was coffee at its purest and tastiest state.

By 1981, Starbucks, with its four locations, caught the attention of a housewares sales representative from New York who wanted to learn why a tiny Seattle coffee company was ordering more coffeemakers than one of the giant national department stores. Howard Schultz was the housewares sales representative, and soon thereafter he parlayed his enchantment for Starbucks into becoming its director of marketing and operations.

In 1983, while on a business trip in Milan, Howard had an epiphany of venti-sized proportions. Enamored with the Italian coffeehouse culture, he envisioned Starbucks selling espresso beverages (caffé lattes and cappuccinos) like the tiny cafes in Italy do. He convinced the three Starbucks owners to try out the coffee-bar concept, highlighting handcrafted espresso drinks, in downtown Seattle. Despite the experiment's success, however, the owners ultimately differed on what Starbucks' business focus should be. Undeterred, Howard left Starbucks to start his own espresso café, Il Giornale, in 1986.

In less than a year, Il Giornale had opened three locations. But serendipitously, in 1987, Schultz was given the opportunity to buy the company that formerly employed him—its six stores and the Starbucks Coffee name. He jumped at the opportunity and began to make reality the company he'd envisioned years before.

By 1992 Starbucks had 165 locations, mostly in the Pacific Northwest, Chicago, and Vancouver, Canada, with annual revenues of $103 million. That same year the company went public. Over the next 14 years, its growth would go wild, at first entering new markets in New York, Los Angeles, and Miami, then opening overseas in Japan, and ultimately becoming not just an instantly recognizable national brand, but an international cultural icon. Starbucks now has more than 11,000 locations—growing at a rate of 5 new stores a day—in more than 40 countries around the world and with revenues in excess of $6.5 billion. Its stock price has increased over 6,400 percent since its initial public offering.

More important to the Starbucks position of being a leading-edge company, however, is that it actually achieved the daunting goal of changing the way people in America—and worldwide—think about and *enjoy* coffee. Starbucks had a mission to change the world. Not simply change *their* world but change *the* world. They wanted to improve people's lives in small but meaningful ways, not just get rich selling stuff. And it is this commitment to serving others that is at the heart of Starbucks' success.

As a brand, Starbucks has redefined modern market-ing by forsaking the traditional marketing trappings of mass advertising and, instead, focusing on building en-dearing and enduring relationships with customers one cup, one store, at a time.

For a company that has accomplished so much, it's surprising how little the business world really knows about how Starbucks found prosperity from selling a com-modity. That's because much of this company's sage ad-vice and weathered truths exist solely in the hearts and minds of longtime Starbucks partners (employees).

Okay . . . so what is *tribal knowledge?* It's the name of the book after all.

Starbucks tribal knowledge is an innate language that has never been written, only spoken, and then, only within the Starbucks tribe. It's a pithy quote by a respected Starbucks executive. It's a mantra used by Starbucks project teams to bring forth passionate followership. It's emotionally intense advice from old-school partners that pierces the souls of new-school partners. It's "a-ha mo-ments" from successful (and failed) projects. It's poignant. It's thought-provoking. It's actionable. It's what built Star-bucks the business and Starbucks the brand.

The tribal knowledge shared in this book is based on unwritten, informal organizational wisdom that infused Starbucks' success and that continues to be passed down from one generation of managers and baristas to the next, coursing through the veins of the Starbucks company cul-ture much like strong coffee invigoratingly courses through one's veins. This book is a collection of those nuggets of tribal wisdom—a written compendium of the truths that, added together, express the learnings and traditions of Starbucks.

There are many roads to success in business. Many businesses focus on price and convenience to attract customers—goods and services are simply a commodity. But in a consumer environment that focuses on delivering these needed commodities quickly, conveniently, and cheaply, with an emphasis on technology and a minimum of personal interaction, there's space for companies that focus on providing an enhanced, more tactile customer experience. Companies that focus on delivering remarkable products and services attract significant attention from customers conditioned to a retail world in which the necessities are bought and sold without fuss or feeling.

Tribal Knowledge is aimed at entrepreneurs and business professionals who embrace that ideal—that products and services can do more than just the minimum—who seek to connect in personal, meaningful ways with customers, who over-deliver on the many promises implied in a typical transaction.

The *tribal truths* discussed in the following pages are business and marketing lessons designed to share ideals and spark ideas you can use to immediately impact your business. Each tribal truth is followed by a number of Leading Questions to prompt you to think about your company and your business practices in different ways. And a short section at the end of the book, From Ideas to

Implementation, suggests a number of action steps you can take to improve your business practices now.

But *Tribal Knowledge* is also more than just a book—it's the beginning of a conversation between you, me, and others. I say this because we have the opportunity to share comments, opinions, and rebuttals on everything written in this book by visiting the Tribal Knowledge blog at *www.tribalknowledge.biz*.

Each tribal truth from the book has its own blog posting, and I encourage you to share your thoughts, whether you noddingly agree or vehemently disagree with the lessons I have shared. I'd love to hear (and others would, too) about how you are using the lessons this book shares to make things happen in your work life.

If you are unfamiliar with what a blog is and clueless as to how to participate in a blog, then this is the perfect time to learn.

In the following pages of *Tribal Knowledge*, you'll gain access to the many business and marketing lessons that helped Starbucks transform the cultural landscape and create an industry from someone who lived inside the Starbucks tribe.

The time has come for people outside the tribe to have access to insider knowledge that helped build the Starbucks business and the Starbucks brand.

A Few Tribal Truths About the

Business of Branding
and the
Branding of Business

Building the Business Creates the Brand

*Managing a brand is a lifetime of work. Brands are fragile.
You have to recognize the success of Starbucks, or any company or
brand, is not an entitlement. It has to be earned every day.*

HOWARD SCHULTZ,

Starbucks chairman and visionary

("Mr. Coffee," Context, August/September 2001, p. 22)

Contrary to what you may have heard or thought, Starbucks never sought to create a brand. Instead, the company passionately sought to create appreciation for a better tasting cup of coffee.

It was, in fact, as basic as that.

The unconscious process of forming its brand came out of unrelenting passion, not unending spin. Starbucks was too busy sourcing and roasting the highest-quality coffee beans to think about *branding*. Starbucks was too busy educating customers on how and why they should appreciate a stronger, bolder cup, more flavorful cup of coffee to think about *branding*. Starbucks was too busy creating a comforting and welcoming place for people to exhale than to think about *branding*.

Starbucks' mission was to change the way people drank and appreciated coffee, and it did this by educating customers about its product with enthusiasm. When the company began, coffee was viewed only as a hot, brown liquid that was consumed out of habit and a need for caffeine. Starbucks knew that the coffee experience could be—and should be—much more than that. When done right, the subtle, rich, exotic flavors of coffee, served in a cozy, relaxing environment could lead to the kind of "rewarding everyday moments" that were missing from the American retail landscape. And so it grew its business by creating knowledgeable customers. It still grows in the same way today—the practices that worked then, work now.

Starbucks positioned its employees (the company calls them *partners*) as the coffee experts because they were. Its baristas learned the craft of serving up a stronger, bolder cup of coffee while chatting with customers, giving the people who came into its stores the opportunity to learn, relax, and enjoy the experience of delicious coffee. And where did the conversation focus? On the beans. Starbucks employees knew backward and forward the story of the coffees they served and easily could rattle off nuances about the roasting process, taste differences between its varietals, blends, and single-origin coffees, and the mystique surrounding the history of the beverages they handcrafted from behind the espresso machine.

It was crucial that Starbucks baristas knew their coffee because Howard Schultz knew that it is all too easy to taint the perfect coffee experience. Even if you select the right beans and roast them to perfection, you can still mess it up in a variety of ways. Coffee beans will retain their peak flavor for only so long (which is why Starbucks donates out-of-date coffee to charity); the grind must be coarser or finer, depending upon the brew (drip coffee versus straight espresso, for example); the ratio of ground coffee to water must be precise; the water must be filtered and pure; the brewing time must be exact (especially for espresso shots); and the brewed coffee must be fresh. With all of this, it's not difficult to see why Starbucks focused more on its coffee and less on its *branding*.

Beyond the coffee itself, Starbucks paid attention to the in-store experience. Store signage at the time looked like travel posters, appealing to customers' adventuresome nature to help explain the origins of the coffees it served. The store itself was clean and uncluttered, keeping the focus on the product and making the atmosphere calm and beckoning.

It was all about the coffee and the experience, never the brand.

But because Starbucks was busy *working on* and *working in* the business, it built a business of which the *by-product* was the creation of a strong brand.

Starbucks teaches us that rarely, if ever, can you sprinkle magical branding dust to create an endearing and enduring brand from scratch. But that doesn't stop companies from trying. Instead of spending money to improve the performance of a product or enhance the customer's experience, many companies will attempt to build a brand by throwing money into multimillion-dollar image campaigns. The focus moves away from product devotion to the *appearance* of product devotion.

A business cannot sustain itself on image, no matter how much money is dumped into sporadic, heavy-up advertising campaigns. Companies that put their money behind their brand and not their business fail to realize that the business *is* the brand. And to realize the full potential of the brand, one must work on and work in the business every day of every year.

You cannot create a brand before you create a business—the process is simultaneous. As you build your business, you create your brand.

Leading Questions . . .

- Does your business define itself by its product or service or by its image?
- How does your business overtly show its passion— its focus—to customers?
- How must your business change to become more business-minded and less brand-focused?

Bake Marketing into Your Business

Brands must do more than provide good products. Today, services and products are the ante. It is how they are positioned and how consumers are engaged that separates the winners from the losers.

SCOTT BEDBURY,
former Starbucks marketing executive
(internal Starbucks presentation, Seattle)

Starbucks has become one of the most respected, admired, and financially successful global businesses in the world without spending a hill of (coffee) beans on advertising. That's amazing when you compare it to companies such as Coca-Cola, Microsoft, and McDonald's, who've spent billions of dollars on traditional advertising campaigns to become global brands.

Yet Starbucks hasn't skimped on marketing itself. Every time it's open for business, its marketing machine is in full effect. It's just that Starbucks has a different view of marketing. As David Packard, cofounder of Hewlett-Packard, once said, "Marketing is too important to be left to the marketing department." Marketing, though a distinct department within the company, is still a part of everyone's job, a part of everything the company does. Starbucks has "baked" marketing into its business by weaving passion for its product into everything it does.

This strategy was intentional from the start, mostly, though, due to the prohibitive cost of advertising. When Starbucks began, it didn't have the cash to advertise because it was putting all the money it had into improving its products and opening more stores. Without the backing of traditional advertising, it had to get creative. And so its in-store experience became Starbucks' primary marketing tool.

Everything about the Starbucks experience marketed the Starbucks business: the coffee in the iconic white logo cup; the personal interaction between a customer and a Starbucks barista; the plush chairs, the in-store color scheme (all themed to reflect the four stages of the roasting story: growth/greens, roast/browns and reds, brew/blues, and aroma/pastels); the music playing overhead; the welcoming smell of the coffee; and the feeling customers had during their Starbucks "moment."

And it worked.

The marketing of the store and the brand has little to do with traditional advertising and everything to do with perfecting the details. Starbucks learned that being conscientious about the little things—and *all* the little things, from how a customer orders a beverage to the cleanliness of its restrooms to the way caramel is drizzled atop a latte—spreads more positive publicity than any television commercial could. And when it came to the product, that's where the company excelled.

Starbucks grew in popularity and expanded geographically based on its willingness to share. They did so by sampling generously: offering its customers the opportunity to taste different coffees on the house. When Starbucks provides samples, it does more so to share than to sell. Yes, it's sharing free coffee, but, more to the point, Starbucks is sharing its passion for dark-roasted coffee and its pride in how the beverage tastes and the craftsmanship that goes into making it. The end result is that its customers receive the entire Starbucks experience firsthand, not through catchy jingles or humorous commercials.

That said, the company did test spending marketing dollars on television commercials in the spring of 1998 to support the increasing popularity of its Frappuccino® blended coffee beverages. Starbucks ended up quickly pulling the campaign, however, because it couldn't immediately measure the impact. But when Starbucks sampled beverages in its stores, baristas could immediately measure sampling's impact by watching the faces (and subsequent smiles) of customers while they tasted the coffee. With the belief that tasting was believing and that the personal touch meant everything, Starbucks cut the TV ads and kept sampling, tapping into its existing customer base to grow sales.

Because word-of-mouth publicity is so integral to the company's success, Starbucks' homespun approaches to marketing go well beyond the immediate in-store experiences customers have. For instance, each Starbucks location is paired with a nearby charity, to which it donates day-old pastries and for which it works to raise awareness and money. And, at the Sundance Film Festival in Park City, Utah, Starbucks acts as a pseudo-sponsor, having set up espresso carts behind the scenes for years. The company doesn't draw much attention to itself by doing these things, but it does know that attention and recognition will come.

In recent years, Starbucks has dedicated some resources to traditional advertising, such as promoting new beverages on billboards and through radio spots, though the efforts are targeted to specific cities, not a national audience. When Starbucks does advertise, it keeps its efforts local and personal, giving everything it has to marketing its business through running its business.

Starbucks learned the most effective way to spend its marketing dollars is not on making funnier television commercials but rather on making better customer experiences. Counterintuitive, yes. But highly successful nonetheless.

Leading Questions . . .

- How does your company's advertising contribute to its sales growth? its mission?
- What role does word-of-mouth publicity play within your company?
- What must change at your company in order for it to spend its marketing dollars not on making the advertising better but on making the customer experience better?

Make the Common Uncommon

Who wants to sell a common, ordinary, everyday, me-too product? More important, who wants to buy one?

The marketplace is chock-full with all-too-similar goods and services in every category imaginable. How many people will actually go out of their way to buy what you're selling if what you're selling is nearly identical to everything else on the market? That's why lasting brand loyalty is built on making the common uncommon—because while a price advantage, or more convenient locations, or whiz-bang product features may vanish tomorrow, uncommon quality attracts and connects with your customers in a powerfully personal and permanent way.

In Guy Kawasaki's classic book on management, *The Macintosh Way*, he expounds on "doing the right things right," part of which is creating the right products. "The right products," he writes, "reward their owners; they are deep, indulgent, complete, and elegant." The products provide everything the customers expect from them, and they satisfy wants, not needs. *Indulgent, elegant*—do these words describe a no-frills transaction? Nope. They describe an experience that is luxurious, perhaps even a guilty pleasure, something a person cannot find just anywhere.

Apple makes the common computer uncommon. Why else would Apple users be willing to pay more and put up with delayed or nonexistent Mac versions of software? They do it because they're unwilling to give up the experience of interacting with their beloved iMacs and iBooks. For Mac devotees and evangelists—not simply "customers"—the advantages far outweigh the disadvantages.

In–N–Out Burger makes the common fast-food hamburger uncommon, offering unsurpassed quality in an industry founded on speed and convenience. Method makes common hand soaps and cleaners uncommon, creating a line of beautifully packaged, sweet-smelling, environmentally friendly products for cost-conscious shoppers. Whole Foods Market makes the common grocery store uncommon, providing a feast for the senses with an in-store atmosphere that compels customers to slow down, sample new foods, and purchase items they probably didn't have on their shopping list to begin with.

And Starbucks makes the common cup of coffee uncommon.

Before Starbucks, the common cup of coffee could best be described as a liquid caffeine-delivery vehicle, a drink to be endured more for its stimulant effects than to be enjoyed for its taste.

Starbucks wasn't satisfied doing coffee as everyone else was doing coffee. Starbucks believed coffee should be enjoyed for its rich, strong, and densely sophisticated flavors and not simply endured for its pick-me-up qualities.

Starbucks would have failed in the marketplace if they positioned coffee as everyone else did—light roast; light flavor; inexpensive, low-grade beans; and cheap, low-impact experiences. Starbucks would have failed if it didn't engage customers with sights, sounds, and surroundings worthy of fostering a cult-like devotion from customers.

Instead, Starbucks has taken the common cup of coffee and made it uncommon by focusing on higher-quality coffee beans, longer roasting styles, and more intense and enjoyable coffee experiences. Starbucks transformed what had once been something to be endured into something to be enjoyed.

Starbucks' almost fanatical insistence on quality— from the beans it selects, the slower, darker roasting process; to the packaging of the roasted coffee beans and the in-store preparation of each cup of coffee, espresso, cappuccino, or latte—has earned the brand a loyalty as intense as its darkest roast. It has also raised the bar. By changing the expectations we have of coffee, it's raised the standards of an entire industry.

But Starbucks refuses to compromise its product in the face of increased competition. Take its roasting techniques as an example. Starbucks was founded with a passion for darker roast coffees. Darker roast means a longer roast; and a longer roast equates to less dense, lighter-weight coffee because more water is extracted from the beans the longer they're roasted. So it takes more roasted beans to fill a one-pound bag of Starbucks coffee than it does for its competitors who package heavier, lighter-roasted beans. And as a result, it costs Starbucks significantly more money and more time to package its coffee beans. The company spends more on this unique aspect of their business and on other things because it's unwilling to sacrifice the quality of a customer's Starbucks experience. This uncompromising passion for quality allows Starbucks to maintain its competitive advantage and the devotion of its customers.

Most companies are resigned to settling for compromise—you can have this *or* you can have that, but you can't have both. It's what Jim Collins refers to in *Built to Last* as the "tyranny of the OR" versus the "genius of the AND." No matter the industry, the most successful, longest-lasting businesses are those that embrace the genius of the "AND" to make the common uncommon.

Leading Questions . . .

- In your category or industry, which company, if any, provides the uncommonly best product or service? If it's not yours, why isn't it and what will you do about it?

- What compromises are you willing to make (and not make) as it relates to the quality of your products and services? Will these compromises diminish your company's ability to deliver an uncommonly good product or service?
- How is your business communicating what it uniquely does so uncommonly well?

Tell the Story.
Don't Make Up a Story.

When businesses tell the story about why their products and services are remarkable, they engage in meaningful marketing.

Meaningful marketing is about designing marketing activities to deliver on the vision of the business all the while being smart, savvy, and authentic. It's about treating consumers as being everyday explorers who seek to be interesting and interested. It's about building preference more than awareness, going beyond capturing attention to soliciting intention, and fostering loyalty beyond reason from customers.

Starbucks has long held that educating customers about the products it offers leads to greater appreciation from customers. Howard Schultz recognized early on that, because of its unique approach to coffee, the company had a compelling story to tell. And when the rest of us thought about where the coffee came from, we realized we had a truly romantic story of hand-picked beans gathered from the slopes of misty hills in far-off places like Kenya and the Indonesian archipelago. It's easy to see the romantic storytelling allure of coffee that travels from exotic mountaintops to our mundane kitchen countertops.

But Starbucks doesn't stop at sharing the bean-to-cup story on its packaging and in-store signs and brochures. It conducts coffee seminars, especially early on during its expansion into new markets, complete with highly-trained and highly-passionate "coffee communication specialists" who talk about the different coffee varietals and suggest appropriate pairings for coffee with various fruits, cheeses, and chocolates. Starbucks views coffee the same way vintners view wine, and it shares its passion with its customers. At one coffee seminar in Denver, held in the public library before the company was a national or even regional mainstay, more than 100 people turned out to learn about coffee from Starbucks—talk about attracting loyal "fans," not simply customers.

These coffee communication specialists—Starbucks' coffee "evangelists"—do more than get *customers* excited about coffee, they also make Starbucks baristas more excited about coffee. By serving as liaisons to store-level baristas, they educate and engage employees to become coffee experts as well.

If your company has a passion for its product, then it has a compelling story to tell and a reason to share so that others can become interested in what fascinates the company to no end.

Unfortunately, when faced with developing marketing programs, many marketers still believe in making up stories about why a product is special. They engage in outrageously gimmicky, attention-grabbing antics that over-promise and woefully under-deliver. These marketers treat consumers as being boring, indifferent, and brainlessly gullible.

The surest way to determine if your marketing is "telling the story" and not "making up a story" is to listen to how your customers are talking about your business. What do they say about your company online? What does the local media say about it? How do your neighbors talk about your company at weekend barbeques? When your marketing is telling the story, customers talk about what your company does. However, when your marketing is making up a story, customers talk about what your company did.

For example, Burger King's recent marketing activities, ranging from the Subservient Chicken Web site to the television commercials featuring "The King," make up stories about the Burger King business. These advertising messages are diversionary marketing tactics designed to get consumers to focus on the kooky, creative commercials Burger King *did* and not on the food Burger King *does*.

Taco Bell does the same thing, but in a much less interesting way—they show, with their TV and print advertising, sizzling hot grills, freshly picked produce, and freshly grated cheese going into their dishes. It's a far cry from the sealed plastic bags containing precooked portions shipped from mammoth distribution centers, which Taco Bell simply heats and serves by tossing the bags into boiling water. It's clear that they've made up a story. Chipotle, on the other hand, makes the food in front of you. You can see the freshness, the quality, and the company reinforces what it does with the story of its marinated meats printed on its cups. It knows there are lots of people with a passion for simple, freshly prepared, and delicious Tex-Mex food, and it over-delivers on the expected fast-food promise.

The big beer companies, Budweiser, Miller, and Coors, also provide a readily familiar example. It's easy to recognize a lack of authentic passion for the beers they produce from their advertising that relies so heavily on the sophomoric interests of young men and other wildly irrelevant diversionary tactics, funny though they often are. When they do attempt to focus on the actual product in their marketing, the vague, often confusing descriptions leave the viewing consumer with precious little to be interested in. Flavor is a hard thing to communicate verbally, but when one beer brand touts having "more flavor"—not malty, rich, hoppy, or sweet, just "more flavor"—and another resorts to claiming it has the "coldest tasting" beer, you know something's wrong. Their approach to beer is akin to how coffee was viewed before Starbucks came on the scene—a cold, foamy, fizzy, yellowish liquid that serves as an alcohol delivery vehicle.

Compare their "stories" to what independent brewer Samuel Adams tells its followers. If you've seen or read their advertising, or noticed the words on their bottles, it's easy to understand what they're all about—better beer. Much as Starbucks paved the way for the specialty coffee industry, Samuel Adams has been at the forefront of the microbrew renaissance of the last 20 years. Samuel Adams did it by being passionate about better beer, and it succeeded in communicating its passion by just telling us its story.

Companies that tell their story in a meaningful and genuine manner become endearing and enduring, while companies that make up stories are fleeting and in seemingly desperate need of attention. Which would you rather have your business associated with: endearing and enduring or fleeting and desperate?

Leading Questions . . .

- What is your company's story? What is it, ultimately, that motivated its founding and exemplifies the passion of its reason for existing?
- How does your company communicate its true, authentic story to its customers and employees?
- In what ways, if any, has it been guilty of "making up stories" in its marketing?

Brand Management Is Reputation Management

Branding is a nebulous term. *Brand* as a noun and *branding* as a verb have different meanings to different people in different departments at different companies.

Because everyone has a different understanding of what a brand is and what a brand does, the Starbucks marketing department views brand management as *reputation management*.

Starbucks marketers have learned that everyone, no matter what department they work in, understands the word *reputation* and all the feelings associated with it. People, places, and things with solid reputations are admired, respected, and trusted, while those with tarnished reputations are viewed as lacking integrity and shunning responsibility.

The same goes for brands. Strong brands are associated with upstanding, character-rich words like "genuineness," "reliability," "virtuous," and "empathetic." While weak brands are linked to dishonorable words such as "insincere," "forgettable," and "shallow."

Measuring the reputation of a brand can and should be as simple as measuring the reputation of a company—something that is earned through purposeful execution and not merely fabricated to exploit a worthwhile business opportunity. Just as the Starbucks brand evolved out of the company's high ideals—more as a by-product of the business than as a prerequisite for company growth—its reputation came about naturally as well. The actions Starbucks took to satisfy its customers, assist its employees, and foster good community relationships all worked toward building a positive company reputation.

Because Starbucks cares about its customers, it treats them as intelligent, discerning individuals. This caring not only shows in its quest to deliver the best coffee possible, but in the peripherals, such as store design. Neighborhood to neighborhood, the store decor changes because the essence of the surroundings changes. A store in Taos, New Mexico, for example, might display works by local artists on its walls, while one in the near south side of Chicago may have a blues theme to it. Yes, the looks are different, but the stores are the same in the way they acknowledge and reflect the culture and interests of the customers they serve.

Because Starbucks cares about its employees, it offers all of them—full-time and part-time workers alike—complete benefits packages, including health care and stock options. And because Starbucks cares about the communities it does business in, it takes an active role in charity involvement, from toy and book drives to fundraisers to sponsoring its employees in local volunteer efforts.

This type of corporate behavior doesn't seem "corporate"; it seems, well, "human," and it earns the respect and trust from customers, employees, and communities. Starbucks' reputation grew by its actions—what it did for people inside and outside the company—not by what it said about itself.

Starbucks marketers have learned that viewing brand management as reputation management goes a long way toward fostering alignment across all business units inside a company as to what a brand is and, more important, what a strong brand can do. And when positive brand reputations are nurtured, they create a virtuous cycle that not only attracts a growing base of customers but quality people who want to become part of, and devoted to, the company.

Leading Questions . . .

- What is the reputation of your business from a customer perspective and from an employee perspective? Do they differ? If so, how and why?
- What could your business do to improve its reputation on both the customer front and the employee front?
- How does your company define its brand? Does the reputation of your company's brand match the reputation of your company?

Creating Category Intrigue Builds Brand Intrigue

Starbucks did not create the specialty coffee category in the United States. But by 1996 Starbucks clearly emerged as the leading specialty coffee retailer. And it established this leadership position not by creating interest in the Starbucks brand, but rather by creating intrigue with the specialty coffee category.

It sounds counterintuitive to promote the category before the brand but, as marketing consultants Al and Laura Ries point out in *The 22 Immutable Laws of Branding*, "Customers don't care about new brands, they care about new categories." Customers looking to be part of the "new best thing" are looking for a totally new experience, not just a new product. In the '80s and early '90s the specialty coffee category was just that—totally new. But for customers to be attracted to the new experience, they had to know about it; for customers to appreciate the category's leading brand, they first had to appreciate the category. Without widespread consumer acceptance of the specialty coffee category, there would be no Starbucks brand to promote.

We can laugh now, but 15 years ago the specialty coffee category was virtually unknown beyond a few coffee connoisseurs. Most of us had never sipped a cappuccino (much less pronounced it) or savored the rich, bold flavor of a single-origin coffee like Sumatra. Most of us drank canned coffee and we liked it (okay, at least we tolerated it).

Before Starbucks could get customers to appreciate and admire its unique brand of coffee, it had to educate them to first appreciate and admire the specialty coffee category. So Starbucks set forth on its mission to educate customers on (1) what the specialty coffee category is, (2) what specialty coffee does, and (3) what specialty coffee aspires to be.

Starbucks promoted what the specialty coffee category is through teaching customers the appreciable differences between canned coffee and specialty coffee. The defining difference, shown especially in early marketing materials and employee training tools, is in the bean itself. Starbucks coffee uses only 100 percent high-quality arabica beans, while canned coffee uses inferior, lower-quality robusta beans. Arabica beans only grow at higher elevations and flourish in the shade. Because they're grown higher, they take longer to grow, which partly accounts for their full flavor. Arabica beans can be dark-roasted to bring out an array of fuller flavors. Robusta beans, on the other hand, can grow in low elevations in full sunlight.

Partly because robusta coffee trees grow quickly, they produce uninteresting, milder tasting coffee than do beans from arabica coffee trees. Plus, robusta beans can't be dark-roasted without becoming burnt and extremely bitter tasting. Fast-growing beans roasted lightly means that costs can be maximized but at the expense of flavor—and maximizing costs (not flavor) is what the canned coffee companies do best.

The specialty coffee category is all about arabica beans. While coffee brewed with arabica beans costs more, the payoff is all in the taste. Starbucks could educate its customers about the differences of their coffees, but only through taste could the customers really ever begin to appreciate specialty coffee and what it could do.

Starbucks promoted what specialty coffee does by having customers taste the difference through sampling. One sip of a freshly brewed cup of Arabian Mocha Sanani and customers immediately knew that this coffee was different from what they drank out of a can—this was coffee they actually *liked*. And after sipping the slightly sweet, roasted nuttiness from a handcrafted caffé latte, customers knew this was something they wanted to experience again and again.

Starbucks showed its customers that coffee could be good, downright enjoyable. It promoted that specialty coffee aspires to be the uncommonly good "everyday coffee." Yes, its cappuccinos and lattes could be viewed as occasional treats, but it is the dark-roasted brew—the "regular" coffee—that could and should kick-start any morning and cap off any evening.

Starbucks shared its pride in its product with customers willing to learn about the specialty coffee category. By promoting the category and creating customer preference for higher-quality, better-tasting coffee, Starbucks became the recognized category leader. After all, a business is not defined by its brand, it's defined by the "category" company it keeps.

Leading Questions . . .

- What leadership role could (and should) your company play in promoting the category it does business in?
- What activities might your business do to build greater customer-appreciation through education?

There's a High Price to a Low-Price Strategy

Building a powerful brand is one part substance and one part emotion. One part science and one part art. We must remember that this is all we do, particularly in our consumer communication.

SCOTT BEDBURY
(internal Starbucks presentation, Seattle)

EDLP is an acronym for Every Day Low Prices. It's a pricing strategy in which companies consistently offer low prices instead of yo-yoing their prices from occasionally being sale-priced to be being priced-to-sell every day.

The retailer most associated with the EDLP pricing strategy is Wal-Mart. And for good reason, they are masters at bringing low prices to market. So masterful that Wal-Mart accounts for nearly 8 cents out of every consumer retail dollar spent in the United States.[1] So masterful that 93 percent of all American households have purchased something from Wal-Mart in the last

12 months.[2] So masterful that Wal-Mart makes $20,000 profit each minute of every day despite working with the slimmest of margins.[3]

It's no question, people flock to Wal-Mart for its low prices.

But people also flock to Starbucks, and Starbucks is nowhere near being the low-price leader when it comes to coffee. In fact, Starbucks has never lowered prices, and it doesn't intend to either.

Healthy profit margins, such as the 90 percent–plus profit margin in every coffee beverage Starbucks sells, afford a company the opportunity to create dynamic customer experiences. Low-price strategies don't do that. Companies with an EDLP affliction are solely focused on cutting costs—that's their only customer draw.

The challenge for a company that chooses to open its doors—and grow its business—based on quality products and services and quality customer experiences is that it has only one shot to make a meaningful customer connection. Customers will overcome their aversion to higher prices if the product or service they are buying is well worth it.

For Starbucks, their one shot was exactly that . . . one shot. The company was—and is—fanatical about quality. For a new customer to buy into the specialty coffee category, to learn what coffee should taste like and be willing to pay a premium for it, that person has to experience a perfect shot of espresso. Intense, dense, and uniquely sweet, a one-ounce shot of espresso serves as the epicenter for most of the coffee drinks Starbucks serves. Back in the day, when more people than not had never tasted anything like Starbucks, every single drink was the company's one shot at success.

This was also a time before push-button automated espresso machines, so each shot had to be meticulously timed by the barista. A busy Starbucks used to be filled with the noises of beeping timers, informing baristas whether or not their espresso shots were perfectly pulled to be served in a customer's beverage. If a shot was pulled outside the 18-second to 23-second span (the time Starbucks believes it takes for brewed espresso perfection), it was dumped right down the drain. No questions asked, none needed—the imperfect shot was dumped. Companies driven by cost-cutting wouldn't think about trashing a product just short of being perfect. But for Starbucks, just short of perfect is nothing at all. One bad shot, one misstep, and the customer might not come back.

Starbucks fiercely protects its pricing power because it knows a low-price strategy is the quickest pathway to commoditizing and marginalizing coffee back to being, well, just coffee. It also knows if it lowers prices, it will have a hard time ever raising them again. Most important of all, Starbucks knows higher prices bring them healthier profit margins, which fuel the cozy experience customers enjoy.

If Starbucks were to lower prices, gone would be the perfect espresso. Gone would be the enthusiastic and energetic barista behind the counter. The music, soft lighting, stylish décor, and plush seating? All gone.

Because of this, Starbucks has never adopted the low-price strategy, but it did make an attempt at discounting items across the board for a time in the 1990s. For a few years, the company offered an annual Friends and Family Discount Day in an attempt to kick-start holiday sales. For one day, all merchandise (except beverages and whole bean coffee) was discounted 20 percent. While it did cause a definite sales spike on that day, it also caused a whole slew of problems. First, it trained customers to expect lower prices. Well-meaning store managers would tip off their most loyal customers that the one-day sale was coming, and employees would graciously hoard product in the back of the store, so merchandise sales suffered significantly in the weeks before the big discount day. On top of this, the sale wreaked havoc on the supply chain. Distribution centers were unable to replenish stores fast enough, and because Starbucks locations do not have a surplus of space for storage, stores couldn't hold enough inventory supply to restock the shelves for the day after the sale. There is no telling how many dollars in sales Starbucks lost during the crucial holiday shopping season because its stores simply didn't have a full array of merchandise to sell following the one-day sale.

So Starbucks lost money on the discount, on the supply-chain strain, and on regular sales leading up to, and following, the one-day sale explosion. The major headache this caused took attention away from the product (the perfect cup of coffee) and what the product could do (enthusiastically satisfy customers), and Starbucks stopped the discount. While it met with some customer dissatisfaction the following year, two years after the company pulled the promotion, the discount was all but a distant memory. Company higher-ups learned from the mistake, and employees and customers turned their focus back to serving and enjoying great coffee at appropriate prices.

If it ever decided to run itself as a priced-to-sell retailer, Starbucks would be admitting it no longer values a unique product or a unique customer experience. Seth Godin, author of *Purple Cow*, goes one step further, saying that a low-price strategy is "the last refuge of a . . . marketer who is out of great ideas." The folks at Starbucks are too smart, too savvy, and too creative to fall for the low-price trap. And if they ever did, Starbucks as we know it—Starbucks as a forward-thinking company—would cease to exist.

Leading Questions . . .

- How many of your marketing programs rely on communicating a low-price strategy?
- How do your customers value the product or service you provide? Do they value its value (low price) or do they value its values (high experiences)?
- How must your business change in order to justify charging customers a premium, margin-rich retail price?

Only Three Strategies Exist to Drive Sales

Let's face it, marketers get paid to overthink everything. Marketers are especially guilty of overcomplicating nearly everything related to increasing sales.

At Starbucks, marketers uncomplicate their work lives by realizing there are three, and *only* three ways a business can increase sales:

1. Get new customers to buy
2. Get current customers to buy more, more often
3. Raise prices

1. GETTING NEW CUSTOMERS TO BUY

Every year, 25 percent of Starbucks' total customer base consists of new customers. These are people who, believe it or not, have never purchased anything at Starbucks

before. They are introduced to Starbucks in many nontraditional ways, including

- a Starbucks opening in their neighborhood;
- a Starbucks opening near their place of work;
- sampling a Starbucks beverage at community
  events;
- hearing a friend rave about the newest and tastiest
  Starbucks coffee beverage;
- wanting to emulate their favorite celebrity whom
  the paparazzi captured sipping from a logo'd Starbucks cup; or
- as mentioned earlier, a friend remarking to them
  about a remarkable Starbucks experience they had.

Starbucks also triggers new customer visitation by expanding its menu offerings to include new coffee beverages and new noncoffee beverages. Coffee will always be
the main draw at Starbucks, but there are significant
numbers of people who either do not like the taste of coffee or do not care to drink coffee for health or religious
reasons. Starbucks caters to these customers by continuously offering noncoffee alternatives, such as blended
iced-tea drinks, blended noncoffee Crème Frappuccino
beverages, and a variety of other options.

2. GETTING CURRENT CUSTOMERS TO BUY MORE, MORE OFTEN

Most businesses think they can trigger more pur-chases from customers by treating them as on/off switches. These businesses attempt to flip the customer switch to "on" through implementing expensive and in-tensive, multidimensional advertising campaigns. In these scenarios, customers are bombarded with myriad marketing messages seen on television, read in print, viewed on billboards, and scanned over the Internet for a prolonged period of time.

Then, the heavy-up advertising stops. Businesses, un-able to sustain the money-draining advertising expenses, essentially turn the customer switch to "off," hoping mar-keting momentum will carry future customer purchases.

Starbucks treats its 40 million weekly customers as volume dials and not as on/off switches because Starbucks "advertises" to customers every day in its stores.

The typical Starbucks customer will visit about six times per month. And every time that customer visits a Starbucks, he and she will be exposed to either sampling of a new beverage or promotional activity highlighting something remarkable happening. This constant hum of remarkable marketing activity creates the virtuous cycle of customers returning more often and customers remark-ing to others about Starbucks more often.

3. RAISING PRICES

The average Starbucks customer spends slightly less than $4 every time he or she makes a purchase. Every few years, Starbucks will raise its prices by a nickel to offset increases in behind-the-scenes costs. These price increases also raise the average amount a customer spends, and that, in turn, drives overall sales.

Customers take Starbucks' price increases in stride and generally do not blush at having to pay a nickel more for their coffee. Immediately following a price increase, Starbucks customer visitation dips slightly, but it rebounds quickly (within a few weeks), and the momentum of increasing its customer base continues.

Another way Starbucks raises prices is by introducing new beverages, many of which are limited-time-only promotional drinks. Pumpkin Spice Latte, Gingerbread Latte, Mint Mocha Chip Frappuccino®, and Toffee Nut Frappuccino® are all examples of new beverages Starbucks has launched in the last few years. Each of these drinks has one thing in common: They are more expensive than a regular latte or a blended Frappuccino beverage.

Businesses can simplify sales strategies by focusing on acquiring new customers; getting current customers to buy more, more often; and/or raising prices. It really is that simple.

Leading Questions . . .

- What changes must your business make to encourage visitation by new customers?
- How might your business increase sales by treating its customers more like volume dials and less like on/off switches?
- How would your customers react to a price increase? What could your business do, or what new product could it create, that would attract customers willing to pay a higher price?

Strong Brands Always Have More Brand Credits Than Debits

The Starbucks marketing research department is kept busy providing oodles and oodles of insights into the Starbucks brand through yearly brand audits. And the company learns a lot from these studies.

However, when it comes to measuring and managing the Starbucks brand on a daily basis, the Starbucks marketing department generally relies on a much simpler method—a brand checkbook.

Just as your personal checkbook has credits and debits, a brand checkbook has credits and debits in the form of brand credits and brand debits. *Brand credits* are business activities that enhance the reputation and perception people have of a brand, and *brand debits* are those that detract from the reputation and perception of the brand.

When faced with determining the appropriateness of marketing activities, such as a promotion, sponsorship, program, or special event, the Starbucks marketing department first determines if the activity is a brand credit or debit.

To determine the positive impact (credit) or negative impact (debit) of a potential marketing activity, Starbucks marketers ask the following questions:

- Does the marketing activity respect the intelligence of Starbucks customers?
- Can Starbucks expertly deliver on all the promises made to customers in the proposed activity?
- Will Starbucks employees be excited and motivated by the activity?
- Will customers view the marketing activity as being clever, original, genuine, and authentic?

If the marketing department answered "Yes" to three of these four questions, then the activity is considered a brand credit.

On the other hand, if Starbucks marketers answered "No" to more than one question, then the activity would be considered a brand debit. The Starbucks marketing department would then need to discuss the business importance of doing the brand debit activity.

An example of a brand-credit marketing activity is when Starbucks wrestled with the idea of running a sweepstakes promotion.

Before Starbucks ran it's first-ever sweepstakes promotion in early 2003, the marketing department had to determine if a sweepstakes promotion was a credit to the brand or a debit to the brand. This particular sweepstakes had Starbucks partnering with Vespa® USA and offering Starbucks customers the opportunity to win a variety of prizes, from trips to Italy to snazzy Vespa® scooters.

The Starbucks marketing department decided this sweepstakes promotion was a brand credit because it was able to emphatically answer "Yes" to three of the four brand checkbook questions.

As it related to respecting the intelligence of Starbucks customers, the marketing department believed the Vespa sweepstakes did so because, not only did it conjure up romantic images of Italy, it also connected Starbucks back to its Italian coffeehouse cultural roots.

The Starbucks marketing department was confident in being able to deliver on all promises made to customers in the sweepstakes because a third-party contest administrator was running the contest, and they would be in charge of making sure all prizes were delivered to the winning customers and ensuring Starbucks complied with the requisite litany of legalities.

Having kicked around the Vespa sweepstakes promotion idea with Starbucks store-level baristas and hearing their excitement for it, Starbucks marketers knew baristas would be jazzed by the promotion.

The one question Starbucks marketers could not emphatically answer "Yes" to was whether or not Starbucks customers would view the marketing activity as being clever, original, genuine, and authentic.

But with three "Yes" answers to only one "No," the Starbucks Vespa Sweepstakes ran, and, by all accounts, it was successful in driving sales as well as surprising and delighting customers with cool prizes.

An example of a marketing activity deemed a brand debit by Starbucks marketers concerns couponing.

Many restaurants and fast-food chains use coupons to drive sales and trials of new products. One common way these businesses coupon is by inserting coupons alongside offers from oil-change shops and dry cleaners in bulk mailings distributed by companies such as Val-Pak. These bulk coupon mailings are an inexpensive way to reach a broad audience.

Starbucks uses couponing but in a very judicious manner. Starbucks has always chosen not to use bulk coupon mailing services because the activity is viewed as being a brand debit more than a brand credit.

Starbucks marketers do not believe inserting a coupon into a bulk mailing envelope respects the intelligence of Starbucks customers. Nor would customers view this particular coupon activity as being clever, original, genuine, or authentic. Internal research has shown Starbucks marketers that its customers expect more originality and for Starbucks to treat them as individuals and not collectively through mass-mailing coupon envelopes.

Furthermore, Starbucks marketers believe store-level baristas would feel de-motivated if they worked for a company that had to resort to such a lowest-common-denominator marketing tactic to goose sales.

Now, just as it is unrealistic for your personal check-book to have only credits and no debits, it's also unrealistic to expect a business will participate only in brand credit marketing activities. But it is vitally important for a healthy, growing business to have more brand credits than brand debits. Otherwise, your brand checkbook will be in a constant state of brand debt. Ultimately, given enough debits, a company will find itself facing *brand insolvency*, a condition that happens when a business continually promises more than it actually delivers, bankrupting the brand. Once this happens, it is extremely difficult to earn back brand credit . . . or customers.

Strong brands, like Starbucks, always manage their business to have more credits than debits in their brand checkbook and so never have to face the threat of brand insolvency.

Leading Questions . . .

- How does your business determine which activities are considered brand credits and which are brand debits?
- If you're not sure how you would determine brand credits and debits, what questions would you have to ask to create a credit/debit measurement tool?
- How might your business incorporate the brand-checkbook measurement model to better measure and manage the marketing activities which impact your business on a daily basis?

Be the Best,
Not the Biggest

*One of Starbucks' greatest challenges is to try to break
the mindset that big can't be good. If we don't, we'll lose the
very values that attracted people to us in the first place.*

HOWARD SCHULTZ
(Pour Your Heart Into It)

Jim Donald, current Starbucks CEO, and Howard Schultz were chatting just before going onstage at the 2004 Starbucks shareholders meeting when Howard remarked to Jim that he couldn't believe Starbucks was about to open its 9,000th location. Jim replied by saying, "Howard, we haven't opened 9,000 locations. We've opened one store, 9,000 times."

It is obvious that Starbucks has been built for growth, but what's not obvious is that Starbucks still acts as if it is growing one store at a time. What is hopefully clear is that Starbucks still maintains its small-company values. When people think of big business, they tend to think of faceless corporations driven by greed and dishonesty that care more about profiting off people than they do about making people's lives more rewarding. But you can't be self-serving while professing to serve your customers.

That's why focusing on being the biggest, as opposed to being the best, undercuts your company's values. Once a company puts its needs—faster growth, increased market share, bigger profits—ahead of its customers, it loses its soul. And it can happen in subtle ways, without anyone even noticing.

In 1996, Starbucks opened its 1,000th location, more than doubling its number of stores from just two years before in 1994. The exuberance of opening new stores in new cities became contagious for everyone working inside Starbucks. A mantra, "2,000 by 2,000," meant to focus the company's mental energy on store growth, began to spread throughout the company, starting first in the corporate boardrooms and spreading deep into backrooms of stores. The objective of the "2,000 by 2,000" mantra was to have Starbucks open 2,000 locations by the turn of the millennium. Although it was a catchy phrase, and Starbucks' growth was related to its mission, it wasn't where the focus ought to have been. Fortunately, because the ingrained culture of Starbucks is so quality-obsessed (and because the goal of 2,000 stores was reached early in 1999), it wasn't difficult to redirect the Starbucks ship back to true north, focusing on making a great cup of coffee and delivering unparalleled experiences to each and every customer.

Just as it never sought to create a brand, Starbucks never set its priority to become the biggest coffee retailer. Starbucks did, however, set out to become the best coffee retailer, trusting that growth would be a by-product of being the best. If the overriding goal had been to be the biggest, Starbucks would have made compromises galore on its quality that it has always been unwilling to make. Growth was and is encouraged, and made possible, by wanting to meet the desires of customers more than wanting to meet sales or profit projections. As Starbucks gains new customers, it wants access to more stores in more convenient places—on the way to the metro train in the morning, near the office after lunch, next to the dry cleaners, just off the Interstate. And Starbucks is determined to be everywhere its customers expect it to be.

The company believes everyone deserves great coffee. And it is this unrelenting desire to share the best coffee with everyone that has truly fueled Starbucks' unparalleled growth.

Starbucks' steadfast drive to become the best coffee retailer has resulted in its being the biggest coffee retailer. It can often work out that way . . . but it never seems to work in the reverse.

Leading Questions . . .

- Review your company's mission statement. Are the stated goals more about quality and excellence than about growth and profit?

- Has your business compromised its values to get bigger? If so, what must your business do to reverse and/or minimize these compromises?
- As your company grows, how do you plan to maintain the focus that led its growth in the first place, both among company leadership, long-time employees, and newly hired employees?

Locationing Is Advertising

"Location, location, location" is the most well-known mantra in the real estate game. Because of Starbucks, it is also becoming a well-known mantra for savvy businesses to receive free advertising exposure.

Locationing is a real-estate—turned universal—marketing strategy where every retail location also serves as a billboard for a business. Everything about a store's physical exterior, from the awning to the logo on the side of the building to the company name in lights, is essentially a billboard communicating the business to customers.

Starbucks locationing strategy is called *Main & Main*, and the real estate department maximizes every opportunity to place Starbucks locations in the most highly visible and highly trafficked street corners—just as advertisers do when selecting billboard sites. Keep in mind that, when Starbucks began growing, this is where the company spent most of its money. Instead of buying billboard space or broadcast air space, Starbucks bought retail space and opened stores. Its creative advertising, through sampling and word-of-mouth coupled with creative locationing, gave it a high-profile presence. That's marketing at its best.

Starbucks continues to place stores with an eye toward marketing itself. It positions its stores to trigger impulse purchases from customers. For example, by locating stores near dry cleaners and video rental stores, it takes full advantage of the commuter traffic generated from people dropping off clothes at the dry cleaners on their way to work and picking up movies from video rental stores on their way home.

The same goes for other specialty food shops. The presence of a Starbucks doesn't mean that local bagel shops, or even mom and pop coffeehouses, will close down. In fact, as Howard Schultz points out in *Pour Your Heart Into It,* a Starbucks store will actually help other businesses like it, bringing more people to the area, educating them on the specialty coffee market, and providing them with another place to get together. And because Starbucks puts great effort into researching prime locations, other businesses often base their own real estate decisions around where Starbucks locates its stores.

The principle around locationing as advertising is basic, and, in most cases, basic works. Location—it's not just meant for the real estate game anymore.

Leading Questions . . .

- What impression does your business location give to your customers?
- How might you better use your business location strategy as a marketing tool to increase brand awareness and drive sales?
- How does the location of your business positively or negatively impact the other businesses around it? How could your business change to cause a more positive impact?

Communicate the Benefit of the Benefit

How can we communicate in an honest way, and crack the code of what this human emotion is without looking like a Tide commercial?

HOWARD SCHULTZ

(internal Starbucks presentation, Seattle)

Marketing 101 teaches us to focus on communicating the benefits—as opposed to the features—when promoting a product. By promoting just the feature—for example, a laptop equipped with wi-fi—a marketer is talking more about the product than the experience. The benefit of having a wi-fi-enabled laptop, Marketing 101 would tell us, is being able to connect wirelessly to the Internet. Great. However, savvy marketers realize that there are a number of layers separating the product feature from the ultimate experience the customer hopes to achieve.

To better engage customers with marketing communication that fosters an experiential and emotional relationship, Starbucks focuses on communicating the *benefit of the benefit* of everything it offers.

In other words, what's the *benefit of the benefit* of the latest Starbucks Hear Music CD compilation featuring emerging and enduring musicians? The benefit of the benefit is that Starbucks customers will become viewed as more the music mavens with their friends because they have been made hip to tasty tunes.

What's the benefit of the benefit of a Gingerbread Latte? Traditional marketing stops at the flavor as the benefit—after all, Starbucks is obsessed with the flavor of its beverages. But what does the flavor really accomplish for the person tasting it. The *benefit of the benefit* of this ginger-and-cinnamon-spiced latte is that its taste will transport the customer to a simpler, more innocent time of holiday glee as only a child can revel in. Starbucks knows its customers don't simply buy a cup of coffee. They buy the *experience* that Starbucks delivers of drinking a cup of coffee in a cozy, relaxing atmosphere. Customers don't just buy a pound of Kenya beans, they buy the feeling of an afternoon around the campfire after a day in safari; they don't merely buy a cup of Breakfast Blend, they buy the laid-back feelings that come with sharing a lazy Sunday morning with loved ones.

The benefit of the benefit puts customers in the place they want to be. It makes the product personal. It's relayed to consumers through the in-store signage, the art on the packaging, the names of the drinks, and the marketing brochures.

But Starbucks goes beyond communicating the benefit of the benefit to just customers—it does the same with its employees. Baristas are trained to talk about coffee in deeply personally ways and not just in basic, literal ways. So instead of using confusing terms like "vibrant acidity" or "elegantly medium-bodied," baristas are taught to describe coffees using the emotional connotations they feel when tasting and smelling coffees. For example, one barista might describe the soothing rich taste of Christmas Blend to a customer in terms of the feeling one gets cuddling up with a fuzzy blanket by a crackling fire while reading a novel. Or another barista might describe the bold and earthy taste of Sulawesi as the perfect complement to an easy going Saturday morning reading the newspaper with John Coltrane's serenading saxophone wafting throughout the house.

It's much more meaningful to personalize a product by highlighting not just its benefit, but the benefit of the benefit.

Leading Questions . . .

- What is the benefit of the benefit of your best-selling product or service? Think about its most important feature and make it more personal, until you've reached the ultimate experience your customers derive from it.

- Review your marketing materials and messages related to your specific products and/or services. Are they communicating product features, product benefits, or the entire personal experience—the benefit of the benefit?

Keep Your Marketing Authentic

Marketing messages surround us consumers no matter where we are and what we do. It's like we are trapped inside a singles bar all day, every day, having to endure pick-up line after pick-up line from a never-ending stream of advertisements hoping to score a one night brand-stand with us.

Starbucks marketers work under the premise that marketing has become the enemy. They believe that consumers today are savvy enough to sniff out anything that smells the least bit insincere and contrived. Marketing authenticity is the antidote to the world being perceived as a gigantic advertisement.

Starbucks marketers use a six-point unwritten code to ensure that the marketing programs they create and implement are authentic, that they're staying on message and on brand, and that they tell the story of what makes the product they are promoting Starbucks-worthy. Ideally, every marketing program created and implemented at Starbucks adheres to the following six unwritten rules:

1. Be genuine and authentic
2. Evoke feelings, never prescribe feelings
3. Always say who you are, never who you are not
4. Stay connected to front-line employees
5. Deliver on all promises made
6. Respect people's intelligence

1. BE GENUINE AND AUTHENTIC

Nothing is more genuine and authentic than brewed coffee. Starbucks believes its marketing messages should be as genuine and authentic as the coffee it brews.

Starbucks has spent a great amount of effort getting to know its customers and what its customers want and expect from the company. This shows in the genuineness of one of their recent co-promotions. In the spring of 2006, Starbucks teamed with the *New York Times* to offer a contest in which customers would purchase a copy of the Sunday paper at a Starbucks store, complete the Sunday crossword within the special Starbucks promotional insert, and send in the completed puzzle after compiling clues over a month-long period. It makes sense that Starbucks would choose to do this over, say, a puzzle contest based on Sudoku or some other super-trendy game. Doing the crossword puzzle over a cup of coffee in Starbucks is just one of the authentic rewarding everyday moments many customers enjoy. This promotion stays genuine by highlighting what many people already come to Starbucks for, and by deepening their interaction with the store. Instead of going the trendy route, Starbucks stayed true to its customers.

And by staying true to its customers, Starbucks keeps its marketing authentic.

2. EVOKE FEELINGS, NEVER PRESCRIBE FEELINGS

Pedantic is not in the vocabulary of Starbucks marketers, so preachy platitudes do not come across in the marketing messages they create. For these marketers, the words and imagery must work together to convey a sense of place, comfort, or mystique.

In fact, far from promoting its own agenda, Starbucks has gone out of its way to foster discussion and discourse in its stores through its "The Way I See It" campaign, in which notable artists, activists, educators, and athletes are quoted on Starbucks cups. The diverse group of voices ranges from Chuck D and Quincy Jones to Deepak Chopra, Rick Warren, Michelle Kwan, and Armistead Maupin.

Launched in 2005, the quotes stir reflection, debate, and in some instances, controversy. The aim is to spark conversation in the old-fashioned coffeehouse tradition that Starbucks has always embraced, and evoking the ideal of a place where ideas are shared. The campaign has since added quotes from Starbucks customers, further enhancing the concept while at the same time getting loyal Starbucks fans involved in the conversation.

3. ALWAYS SAY WHO YOU ARE, NEVER WHO YOU ARE NOT

When a business says who they are *not* in marketing materials, they are actually saying more about their competition than they are about themselves. You'll never see Starbucks referring to its competitors in any of its promotional materials. The company doesn't want to bring any attention to the competition. So while Starbucks will tout the high qualities of its newest Frappuccino blended beverage, for example, it will not advertise why its cold, creamy coffee drink is better than what's being offered by other coffeehouses. While you will see Starbucks mentioning that it sources, roasts, and sells Fair Trade Certified™ coffees, it purposely chooses not to compare its Fair Trade coffees with other coffee retailers who sell similar Fair Trade coffees. By doing this, the company keeps the attention where it wants it: on itself.

4. STAY CONNECTED TO FRONT-LINE EMPLOYEES

Starbucks believes if an employee doesn't respect or feel connected to a marketing program, then customers will not either. After all, Starbucks relies on its front-line employees to communicate its marketing messages to customers. And if front-line employees cannot connect with the marketing program, they will not make connections with customers about it.

Every November, when Starbucks releases its heavily anticipated Christmas Blend coffee, it's an important time for stores and employees, who get an immediate increase in demand for the popular blend. Starbucks store managers can always expect a voice mail from Howard Schultz on the morning that Christmas Blend is launched. He'll leave the message from his Seattle home early in the morning, after having just brewed a batch on his French press, and share memories of what the holidays mean to him, his family, and the company.

The voice mails are one way that Howard communicates something deeper—about the coffee, the experience, and the company's roots—to Starbucks employees. In 2002, as the company's endeavors started embracing so many new things extending well beyond coffee, Howard took to leaving monthly voice mails to all stores sharing stories about his favorite coffees in order to return the focus of coffee to front-line employees. Other company leadership in the various regions followed suit, using voice mail, rather than simply typing an e-mail, to communicate the feeling and tone behind the experience Starbucks tries to impart to customers through coffee. By sharing their enthusiasm and their enjoyment, Howard and the other company executives highlight for the front-line staff the *why* of what they're all doing, not just the *how*.

5. DELIVER ON ALL PROMISES MADE

Nothing will turn customers off more than promising something and not delivering. Authentic marketing is strictly tied to this, and it applies to everything that's promised, from supporting local charities, to offering benefits to all employees, to providing the perfect shot of espresso. Starbucks adheres to this right down to the photos of drinks it displays. Marketers at Starbucks would wince seeing a pristine-looking beverage on in-store signage. Take a look at a sign next time you're waiting for your barista to hand you your drink. For a sign featuring Marble Mocha Macchiato, as an example, even the chocolate drizzle lattice pattern on the foamed milk will be just a little bit off. The company wants its signage to look real, slightly imperfect, as if a barista just finished making it. And knowing that no human could ever perfect the chocolate drizzle lattice pattern, the sign reflects that.

Contrast that to what you see in fast-food advertising: the thick hamburger patty covered with red-ripe tomatoes, and leafy lettuce, and thick-cut onions on a fresh-from-the-oven bun. Does it look too good to be true? Usually yes. But once you've taken the paper off and found a smashed burger with a yellowish tomato slice, wilted lettuce, scant onions, and a tissue-thin hamburger patty, you've already given your money to the restaurant. You could complain, but you'll only be rewarded with more of the same. For these companies, marketing is a way to lure customers, and what happens after they've ordered really doesn't matter. Sadly, we've come to expect this.

For Starbucks, marketing is a way to get customers to try new things and feel better about themselves—it's the overall experience, the realness of the product, that matters most. For Starbucks, it's all in the details of reality.

6. RESPECT PEOPLE'S INTELLIGENCE

Starbucks treats customers as being interesting to get them interested. And interesting people, as Starbucks sees them, are constantly expanding their knowledge and horizons. For this reason, Starbucks uses a more educated approach when it speaks to its customers, from how it talks about itself as a company to the level of detail on its packaging. Starbucks consistently views coffee much like wine. Wine enthusiasts have acquired a palette for the various varietals and blends. They have an appreciation for the finer things and usually are willing to put their money behind their interests. Just as a wine label will talk about where the grapes were grown and the flavors elicited in that first sip, Starbucks whole bean packaging talks about the coffee region and the roasting process.

An educated customer still has one final step to go: the ordering process. Starbucks respects its customers' intelligence by not posting signs around the store with "Venti = Large, Grande = Medium." While it may take a little longer to figure out how to order your double tall, half-caf, vanilla, nonfat latte, once you do, there's a feeling of belongingness, that you're part of the "club."

That's the same reason Starbucks doesn't offer combo deals, like nearly every other quick service fastfood restaurant does. It wants the customer to be able to order on her or his own. But no company can ever be perfect. One time Starbucks stores displayed a countertop sign at its registers promoting its version of a combo deal—"A Perfect Pair": a scone and a cup of coffee. These signs were prominently featured in stores, that is, until Howard Schultz saw the sign in one of his stores and trudged back to company headquarters, with the repulsive sign in hand, calling for the complete removal of the counter card sign. The signage creative didn't respect customers; it spoke like a fast-food retailer; it wasn't true to the company. The signs were pulled immediately from all stores as Starbucks marketers realized that the promotion strayed far from their unwritten rules of marketing authenticity.

Building a brand and growing a business that stays true to itself is not about perfection but progress, about being capable of recognizing missteps and then fixing mistakes. That progress is what keeps strong companies moving forward.

Leading Questions . . .

- What does your company do to ensure your marketing materials reflect the company's mission and innate integrity?
- How does your company address its competition in its advertising? Does it speak to the value of your product or does it speak to the lack of value from your competitors?
- How does your company respect the intelligence of its customers?

Keep Your Merchandising Relevant

While representing slightly less than 10 percent of a store's total sales, merchandise at Starbucks still plays an important role of complementing and accentuating a customer's coffee experience. Thanks to Starbucks, stainless steel tumblers have become an indispensable accessory for commuters of all types.

Over the years, Starbucks has experimented in its merchandise strategy with varying results. Translucent dustpans didn't sell. Neither did fancy pencil sharpeners, nor did T-shirts. But Italian-made ceramics have sold very well, as have board games such as Cranium®.

Because Starbucks is viewed as a taste-maker, competing coffee businesses (and Starbucks customers, for that matter) seek to understand why the company chooses to sell the selective merchandise it does.

Selecting the right merchandising assortment is risky, but Starbucks reduces the inherent risks by adhering to the following five unwritten merchandise relevancy guardrails:

1. Merchandise quality matches the high quality of Starbucks coffee.
2. Merchandise links directly to coffee or to a "coffee moment."
3. Starbucks can make the product uncommonly better by adding innovation and or unique style.
4. The product offers distribution opportunities outside of Starbucks stores, such as grocery stores, online, etc.
5. The product provides customers "rewarding moments," be it in a Starbucks store, in a customer's home, at a customer's place of work, or while a customer is on the go.

Leading Questions . . .

- What does your company do to ensure your merchandise is relevant to its product? Guardrails? Gut instinct? Combination of the two?
- Given Starbucks' merchandise guardrails, which ones might you add, delete, or modify to better address your business merchandising opportunities?

Actions Speak Louder Than Advertising

Excessive marketing spending will only accelerate the demise of any poorly conceived company.

SCOTT BEDBURY
(A New Brand World: 8 Principles for Achieving Brand Leadership in the 21st Century)

For many marketers, the answer to the question of, "Sales are down, what should we do?" is to spend marketing dollars on creating an advertising campaign. Not at Starbucks.

During its formative growth years from 1987 to 1997, Starbucks spent less than $10 million on advertising—for a publicly traded retailer the size of Starbucks, that kind of miniscule advertising expenditure is almost unheard of, especially for a growing brand. (Consider that in 2006, a 30-second spot that aired during Super Bowl XL cost $2.5 million. Coke and Pepsi each go through $10 million on advertising expenditures in about two or three days. Their extravagance makes Starbucks skimpy advertising outlays all the more remarkable, doesn't it?)

When Starbucks was young and developing, it eschewed advertising more as a matter of not being able to afford it than anything else. But as Starbucks grew, building its business and its brand in concert, it realized something significant: Word-of-mouth was the best advertising any company could ever hope to receive. And, despite the fact that many marketers are now figuring out ways to "buy" this kind of buzz from consumers, the most effective word-of-mouth advertising still can't be bought. Even if you're telling your story, and not making it up, your advertising efforts will increasingly meet skepticism in a marketplace saturated with competing and boisterous advertising messages. The bottom line is this: You still have to be remarkable if you want to get remarked about.

Seth Godin, in his book *Purple Cow,* illustrates the new, post–"TV-industrial-complex" marketing model by contrasting the examples of the success of Volkswagen's original Beetle and its redesigned new Beetle. The original Beetle languished in the United States for years before Volkswagen (VW) hooked up with the forward-thinking advertising agency Doyle Dane Bernbach in 1959, and launched one of the most significant and effective print and TV campaigns of the 20th century. Forty years later, when VW redesigned their by-then retired Beetle model, it didn't rely on advertising to convince people to buy the car. It put its attention into the sleek, rounded design of the exterior and the car's sporty handling. Genuine enthusiasm from industry press and customers who spread the word created credible buzz and, combined with the car's distinctive, irresistible look, made it the one car everyone *wanted*. "Every time the very round Beetle drove down a street filled with boxy SUVs," Godin writes, "it was marketing itself."

Marketers face a brave new world of satisfying consumer wants, not needs. And, increasingly, advertising has less of an impact on people's consciousness than it used to. The louder and more frequent the messages become, the more people tune them out.

The Starbucks marketing department practices an agnostic attitude about advertising more than an atheistic attitude. That is, it's not impossible that Starbucks would never, under any circumstances, believe in advertising. It's just that the company has its doubts, and it is not willing to commit to having faith in advertising to make sales happen.

Again, it's not that Starbucks doesn't believe in *any* advertising. It's just that the company knows there are much more effective ways to drive sales and build its brand.

Marketing at Starbucks is more a case of doing and being rather than saying. Starbucks would rather *do what they do* and *be who they are* and not succumb to using traditional advertising to say what they do and say who they are. Instead, Starbucks would rather spend marketing dollars to make the customer experience better and not to make the advertising better.

Starbucks spends its marketing dollars to make the customer experience better by

- adding more unique beverages to its menu;
- adding wireless internet (wi-fi) and music listening/CD-burning kiosks to the coffee experience;
- adding more comfy couches and more reading tables in its stores; and
- adding more partners on staff to increase speed of service to customers.

All of the business activities mentioned above are considered marketing activities to Starbucks because a customer's experience is "the marketing" for Starbucks.

Customers have told Starbucks its image of authenticity and integrity has been enhanced by its limited use of traditional advertising. Many Starbucks customers hold the belief that traditional advertising shouldn't be trusted, that it is an unnecessary marketing activity for Starbucks to engage in.

For Starbucks, action, not advertising, is the most effective way to drive sales and build a brand.

Leading Questions . . .

- What goals are your advertising campaigns trying to meet? Are you counting on advertising to build your brand in ways that might be better accomplished

through improving your products and/or services
and enhancing customer experiences?

- If you freed up advertising dollars to be spent elsewhere within your marketing budget, how best
  would you allocate the money to focus more on
  being and doing rather than *saying?*

TRIBAL TRUTH 16

Fewer, Bigger, Better
Is Best

Admittedly, Starbucks is still learning this lesson of doing fewer things to realize bigger, better results. For years the internal mantra has been "Unplug Before Your Plug." This means: Before Starbucks was to launch a new beverage or initiate a new marketing program, a beverage would have to be removed from the menu or a marketing program would have to fully run its course.

This unplugging thing at Starbucks hasn't gone as planned.

Ten years ago, the menu at Starbucks was much simpler, but customers could still customize their coffee drink in one of 10,000 ways. Today, the beverage menu has exploded, and now there more than 55,000 different ways a customer can personalize their Starbucks beverage. Plus the marketing team is stretched thin managing wide-ranging partnerships with the likes of Yahoo!, Lions Gate Films, Jim Beam, and so on.

Yet there are still so many more worthwhile initiatives Starbucks could participate in—but the company says no to 99.5 percent of all the programs proposed to them.

Starbucks is full of passionate overachievers eager to take on every worthwhile project. And with a never-ending stream of seemingly worthwhile projects always on the to-do list of Starbucks marketers, many have to remind themselves that fewer, bigger, better is still best.

The Starbucks marketing culture teaches that focusing on fewer marketing programs will result in building bigger programs, and bigger programs will ultimately drive better results.

As Starbucks moves forward, it remains to be seen how well it can manage this philosophy. Their "Ultimate Coffeehouse Crossword Challenge" contest promotion with the *New York Times* adhered to the marketing guidelines in every way and garnered the desired results. Yet Starbucks' promotion of the Lions Gate film *Akeelah and the Bee* may have compromised some of the company's hard-earned integrity. As movie tie-ins go, it was certainly a far cry from the typical fast-food chain–Hollywood blockbuster cross-promotion. An independent, feel-good movie about an 11-year-old African-American girl competing in the National Spelling Bee, *Akeelah* probably appealed to the archetypal Starbucks customer. And Starbucks' promotion of the film cost the company next to nothing, yet garnered a share of box office sales (albeit small as it was), merchandising revenue, television rights, soundtrack sales, and DVD sales—millions of dollars in revenues that went directly to the bottom line. In other words, the financial risk was nonexistent, while the financial upside was tremendous.

But what of the downside in terms of violating the trust of Starbucks customers and employees? Because the promotion had little to do with the customer experience, people may have felt as though they were being used as pawns in the marketing game.

I think Starbucks would argue that there is a benefit to its customers, in that it clues them into a worthwhile, thought-provoking, and inspirational film—a parallel to what it's doing with music. But it does seem perilously close to violating its own rules of marketing promotion, and it is one more thing added to the mix. It's doing more, not fewer, bigger, or better. Will it have been worth it in the long-run? Ultimately, it may or may not be a trade-off Starbucks is willing to make again in the future.

The innate culture at Starbucks understands that you become more effective by being more selective. You cannot expect to succeed when you attempt to implement multiple marketing programs at the same time. Customers will be confused, and you will become exhausted trying to manage everything.

Leading Questions . . .

- How do your customers and employees respond to your promotions? Are there too many to keep track of? Is each program significant enough to make an impact? And do they align with the experience(s) you're selling?

- If you look at your marketing programs, from the present back to 12 months ago, which ones are memorable? Which ones are customers and employees still talking about? Would eliminating half of them have been unthinkable? Or would it have been easy, in retrospect?

A Goliath Can Become a David Again

A company can grow big without losing the passion and personality that built it, but only if it's driven by values and by people, not by profits.

HOWARD SCHULTZ

(John Simmons, My Sister's a Barista: How They Made Starbucks a Home from Home, Revised Edition [UK], Cyan Communications, 2005, p. 245.)

There is a life-cycle model called the Sigmoid Curve, a leaning-forward S, that describes the stumbling beginning, fast rise, glorious peak, and slow decline of every successful business, brand, or even idea. Management guru and author Charles Handy discussed this model in his book, *The Age of Paradox*, and pointed out that the right time to create a new idea, start a new curve, is when you are approaching the apex, not once you have passed it—for once you start down the other side of that curve, it may be too late, as illustrated in the diagram on the next page.

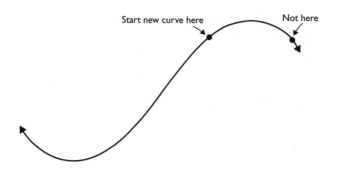

Sounds simple, but how to do that in the real world? Once you're on your way to becoming a Goliath, do you really want to go through being a David again? It may be more romantic, but let's remember, David was the underdog—and for good reason. But if you settle into the summit of the curve, you're a Goliath just waiting for the next David to come along and knock you off your perch.

Starbucks long outgrew being the David of the specialty coffee industry and became its Goliath. The company dwarfs all specialty coffee competitors in market share and customer "mind share." However, Starbucks refuses to settle into the role of being a coffee Goliath. It will not consider itself a Goliath because it no longer considers other coffee retailers as its competition.

Starbucks began with the mission of wanting to get the world to appreciate better tasting coffee. To put it simply, Starbucks has accomplished this mission. With the popularity and sustainability of the company, the next step is to make the transition from Starbucks as coffee "brand" to Starbucks as beverage "icon." From this perspective, Starbucks is an upstart, competing against the old-school beverage icons like Coke and Pepsi. Starbucks considers itself a David because, compared to Goliath-proportioned Pepsi's $30 billion and Coke's $22.5 billion yearly revenues, its annual $6.5 billion is a blip in the megalithic beverage industry machine.

So what is Starbucks doing to step up to its new self-imposed competitors? One way is to look to other brand icons for ideas. Take Coke's Diet Black Cherry Vanilla Coke® beverage and compare that to the Starbucks Marble Mocha Macchiato. Both rely on what started as a specialized drink (Vanilla Coke® and a Caramel Macchiato) and then grew into enhanced versions of themselves. And, taking a page from iconic McDonald's and its "limited-time only" specials like the McRib® and the Shamrock Shake®, Starbucks has introduced promotional holiday beverages. Drinks such as the Pumpkin Spice Latte and the Peppermint Mocha bring a higher price point and add some zest to the usual menu offerings for customers, and that translates into driving higher year-over-year sales at Starbucks.

Sure, borrowing some sales gimmicks from the large competitors works to some extent, but Starbucks didn't get where it is today by following other companies. Its brand is strong because it is the leader in the specialty coffee industry, and it led because of the passion its people had for the product. To transition to icon status will take

hard work, significant investment, and continued passion. Upping the ante, going up against the Goliaths on a
bigger stage, gets company adrenaline flowing. It moti-
vates employees to keep a competitive edge, especially
when the competition has changed. Nobody roots for Goliath. Most everybody roots for David. The best companies have their own employees rooting for them. Getting
bigger by positioning itself as being smaller can rally customers and employees alike.

Starbucks' success turned Starbucks into a Goliath,
and now it has redefined and repositioned itself against
a bigger Goliath in order to become a David again—a
position Starbucks feels much more motivated operating
under.

Leading Questions . . .

- Who are the Goliaths and the Davids within your
  company's competitive set?
- How must your business change to maintain its
  upstart David mentality no matter how big your
  business gets?

DUE

Some Tribal Truths About

Delivering Memorable Customer Experiences

Remarkable Things Get Remarked About

When it comes to delivering memorable customer experiences, Starbucks follows "The Law of Remarkability." This little-known, rarely followed marketing principle simply states *remarkable things get remarked about*. Because Starbucks strives to deliver memorable experiences, customers are more likely to tell their friends and family about Starbucks' remarkability.

For Starbucks, it has been far more meaningful to get customers to tell their best friends about the beverages and coffees they enjoy from Starbucks than to try and convince them with a television commercial or advertising campaign. That's genuine word-of-mouth at its best— when customers willingly, without artificial prodding from advertisers, talk about products and services they believe are worth talking about.

Word-of-mouth is a powerful tool. In fact, many studies show that word-of-mouth marketing is the most influential marketing medium in effecting consumer purchase decisions, ranking ahead of traditional advertising (television, radio, and print) and nontraditional marketing (couponing, online advertising, and in-store promotions). But to get customers to engage in word-of-mouth marketing, companies need to create products, services, and experiences that are worth remarking about. As Seth Godin writes in *Purple Cow:* "In a busy marketplace, not standing out is the same as being invisible." The only reason customers will tell their friends about your great product is if your product really deserves the attention.

Starbucks taps into word-of-mouth marketing through being remarkably different because being remarkable is the one element it can control. By its very nature, word-of-mouth cannot be controlled—only sparked. Just as gossip between two people cannot be controlled, neither can word-of-mouth recommendations. Customers will say what they want, when they want, where they want, and for whatever reason they want. No, word-of-mouth marketing cannot be controlled, but it can be sparked. When Starbucks provides great coffee experiences by giving its customers a customized coffee beverage along with personal, attentive service, it sparks real, unplanned conversations between customers and their friends. In a way, it's a classic case of "I'll have what she's having" working to Starbucks' best advantage.

Back in the spring of 1995, Starbucks introduced the creamy and cold Frappuccino® blended beverage. The wild success of the Frappuccino spread solely via word-of-mouth because the drink was worth remarking about—there was essentially nothing else like it being offered on the scale at which Starbucks was offering it. Not only did the icy cold sweetened coffee concoction appeal to the coffee-drinking masses, it also appealed to those who had sworn off coffee because it tasted too much like, well, coffee. And that's what was so remarkable about the Frappuccino and had people remarking about it—it appealed to nearly everyone, coffee drinkers and non-coffee-drinkers alike. Word-of-mouth marketing for the beverage began in-store with customers taking their first sip. "Wow! Never imagined coffee tasting this good" was the general sentiment from those discovering Frappuccinos for the first time. Other customers waiting in the back of the line would witness this unbridled reaction from first-time Frappuccino drinkers, and, when it was their turn to order, they would say something like, "I'll have what she's having."

Clearly the successful launch of the Frappuccino was buoyed by this domino effect of ordering that occurred from customer to customer and store to store. Plus, word-of-mouth for Frappuccino happened outside Starbucks as well, with current customers happily sharing the news Starbucks now had a beverage their non-coffee-drinking friends would enjoy.

The next year, 1996, Starbucks celebrated its 25th anniversary by introducing another indulgent, sweet-tasting, mass-appealing drink: Caramel Macchiato. While the domino effect of in-store word-of-mouth helped drive sales of the new drink, it wasn't until the fall of 1998 when Meg Ryan's character in the film *You've Got Mail* ordered one, that the Caramel Macchiato really took off in popularity. While customers could hardly pronounce Caramel Macchiato, Starbucks baristas all knew the motivation behind their order came from seeing *You've Got Mail*.

This sounds like the usual product placement you'd expect from a large corporation as a result of an expensive, yet deftly crafted, marketing ploy convincing a Hollywood producer to integrate certain brands into the show, but it's not. Starbucks didn't pay for product placement in *You've Got Mail*. Nor did Starbucks pay for the numerous mentions and logo'd cup sightings on *Ally McBeal* or *Sex in the City*. Nor did Starbucks dole out dollars for its prominent role in the first two Austin Powers movies. Instead, the producers of these shows came to Starbucks specifically because they wanted to borrow some of 'Starbucks' juju to enhance the public's understanding of the characters in their productions. In *The End of Advertising As We Know It,* Sergio Zyman explains this marketing strategy by writing, "If your brand doesn't already conjure up the images and associations you want consumers to get when they think of your brand, then you'll need to borrow those qualities from someone or something that already has them."

While Starbucks doesn't pay outright product placement fees, it will many times open a kiosk on the sets of television shows and feature films to keep the cast and crew pleasantly caffeinated. This kiosk placement not only sets up a cleverly disguised marketing strategy, but it can start a word-of-mouth message that starts on the lips of actors performing on-screen and ends up on the lips of customers ordering at Starbucks. With the right product, the right message can be spread from anywhere to anyone.

Of course, without a remarkable product, even good advertising can't sustain customer interest. Starbucks has the confidence it's delivering customers the best coffee moment possible, and it puts faith in its customers to appreciate the value of the experience enough to stay interested visit after visit and year after year. Starbucks doesn't tell its customers what to say to one another and to their friends, it gives them a great experience and the responsibility of relaying that experience to whomever they see fit. The company trusts its customers because it trusts its products will deliver.

Starbucks has shown the business world that by following the Law of Remarkability, remarkable awareness and remarkable appreciation can be built. (Oh yeah, and remarkable sales success can follow, too.)

Leading Questions . . .

- What is it about your company's product that makes it stand out from all others in its competitive set?
- What ideas do you have to apply the "Law of Remarkability" to your business?

- If your company abandoned all traditional advertising, would your product still succeed on word-
  of-mouth? If not, what can be done to make your
  products and services word-of-mouth worthy?

Needs Are Rational. Wants Are Aspirational.

My highest aim is to have the entire Starbucks experience provide human connection and personal enrichment in cherished moments, around the world, one cup at a time.

HOWARD SCHULTZ
(internal Starbucks presentation, Seattle)

Everyone aspires to live a certain lifestyle, but most times they settle for living a life below their aspirations. Starbucks understands that an aspirational gap exists between the lifestyle most consumers aspire to live and the actual lifestyle they do live. Knowing this, Starbucks strives to help people actualize their aspirations of having human connection and personal enrichment.

By tapping into people's wants and offering them a way to actualize their aspirations, businesses can transcend the commoditization trap. Successful businesses find ways to close the aspirational gap by fulfilling consumer wants, not needs. The discount chain Target, with its "expect more, pay less" business mindset typifies this principle beautifully. Target satisfies its customers' needs of affordability while fulfilling their aspirations to have stylish decor and fashionable clothes. Target has tapped into its customers' beliefs that style doesn't have to come at a high price and, in turn, has acquired a mass of loyal customers for it.

However, most businesses resort to only fulfilling consumers' needs and not their wants. Marketers at these businesses will typically develop products and programs to strictly solve for a particular consumer "need-state." For instance, creating and launching a new drink to fulfill a consumer's thirst-quenching need. Or a new flavor-line extension of a commonplace product to fulfill a consumer's need for a different yet similar taste appeal.

Needs are basic. Needs are rational. Needs are boring. Needs have been commoditized. Every unremarkable business seems to be in the needs-fulfilling business.

Wants are emotional. Wants are aspirational. Wants are thrilling. Wants are where the profits are. Only truly remarkable businesses are in the business of satisfying customer wants by helping customers actualize their aspirations. These companies give their customers the feeling that no expense was spared. Whether they are selling luxury cars, gourmet meals, or $4 cups of coffee, businesses that fulfill their customers' wants help their customers to live the life of their dreams.

Despite Starbucks being so convenient—it's opening new stores at a rate of five a day somewhere in the world—people still place a high value on it, and that value is all about "wants." No one needs a Caramel Macchiato from Starbucks. No one needs a Starbucks Cinnamon Dolce Frappuccino® blended beverage. And no one needs to spend time reading a newspaper in one of Starbucks' comfy chairs. No one needs the extras in life, but Starbucks knows that the extras are what its customers crave and deserve. By serving them great coffee, personalizing their experience, giving them a chance to take a break from fulfilling the real needs in their lives, Starbucks offers its customers a pampered moment. With this feeling of privilege comes the closing of the aspirational gap. For the seconds the customer is transported in that first sip or the minutes spent relaxing in an overstuffed chair, aspirations have been reached (even if it is merely a fleeting feeling). This is the feeling, the want, that keeps customers coming back.

Leading Questions . . .

- Make a distinction between your own needs and wants. How do the stores you shop at and the companies you do business with fulfill your needs versus your wants? How many of those companies do both?
- Compare and contrast the basic needs of your customers with their aspirational wants. Where does your business help to close the aspirational gap for its customers?

Say Yes to Connecting, Discovering, and Responding

As long as it is moral, legal, and ethical,
we should do whatever it takes to please the customer.

HOWARD BEHAR,
former Starbucks executive

While it does serve up a great cup of coffee and pull the perfect espresso shot, Starbucks keeps its customers in the store by providing uplifting experiences and enriching their daily lives. Its customers have come to expect a connectedness to the store—through groovy music and a relaxing atmosphere—and to the baristas. Starbucks focuses much of its store-level barista training programs on teaching employees to deliver not ordinary customer service but legendary customer service. However, Starbucks doesn't totally rely on bulky and verbose training manuals to teach baristas how to deliver legendary customer service. Instead, Starbucks instills two customer-service-focused

mantras in the hearts and minds of every barista: "Just Say
Yes" and "Connect, Discover, Respond."

JUST SAY YES

Yes is one of the most optimistic, courteous, and actionable words in customer service. It's also one of the
easiest ways Starbucks has found to create enthusiastically satisfied customers. For those reasons, Starbucks baristas are trained to just say "Yes" to customer wants.

The attitude of "Just Say Yes" has had a big impact on
Starbucks' offerings beyond merely being friendly. In the
late 1980s, as Howard Schultz was growing the company's
nascent coffee shops into a national success, Starbucks was
still tightly tethered to its roots as a provider of "authentic" coffee drinks. Using Italian coffee bars as the model,
Starbucks offered its lattes and cappuccinos with only
whole milk. Howard Schultz wrestled with the decision to
offer customers nonfat-milk options, feeling anything besides whole milk would dilute the perfect latte. Howard
Behar, who was in charge of running retail operations at
the time and whom Schultz credits for creating Starbucks'
customer service ethos, urged Schultz to reconsider. It
wasn't until Schultz saw a single customer walk away from
Starbucks for not being able to have her cappuccino prepared with skim milk that he changed his mind. The loss
of one customer in one store might not matter to most
already profitable companies, but to Starbucks it makes all

the difference. Now, many years later, it is interesting to note nearly half the drinks ordered by customers at Starbucks are made with nonfat milk.

Going one step further, if a customer, for whatever reason, voices displeasure with her espresso drink, Starbucks' customer service culture calls for a barista to "Just Say Yes" and do whatever it takes to right a wrong—this usually means remaking the drink on the spot.

By saying "Yes" to customers, you automatically focus on what you are able to do and not what you are unable to do. Starbucks has found that when baristas answer "Yes" to customer requests, it opens up a more welcoming and gracious path to delivering out-of-the-ordinary customer service.

CONNECT, DISCOVER, RESPOND

Delivering legendary customer service at Starbucks is not about acting. It's about *reacting*—reacting to customers' expectations, voiced and unvoiced.

Baristas are taught to make connections with customers through either simply acknowledging the customers' presence when they enter the store or through engaging in casual, friendly conversation. During this connection, baristas are looking and listening for clues to discover their customers' needs. A good barista will remember his and her regular customers either by name or by drink and be able to have their "usual" in queue just as they walk in the door. A good barista will anticipate when stressed-out businesspersons need an extra heaping of whipped cream on their mocha or which flavored latte newcomers would like. A good barista will deliver an order to the table of a dad with his hands full with his kids or to a woman with her hands full of paperwork.

After making a connection and discovering a need, the barista's ability to respond accordingly will bring smiles to the faces of the customers and will keep them as regulars.

Leading Questions . . .

- List the ways in which the employees on your business's front lines connect with your customers. Is making meaningful customer connections built into your company's corporate culture? If not, why not?
- Does your company have policies in place that restrict employees' ability to say "Yes" to customers? If so, how can you change this?

Over-Deliver on All Promises

When businesses follow through on the promises they've made to their customers, they're displaying an integrity that's necessary to building trust between customers and the brand; and they're also showing a pride in the work they do—the products they make and the services they deliver. Ultimately, how a company follows through on its promises is more a reflection of who that company is and its reason for existing than anything else. A company that delivers what it claims it will is simply treating its customers exactly the way it would like to be treated.

Starbucks makes promises to customers every day. Whether it's the promise of serving a fresh cup of coffee or preparing a beverage with the perfect shot of espresso in a timely manner, Starbucks strives to fulfill its promises every day.

But delivering on promises is not enough today. Businesses, big or small, must find ways to over-deliver on their promises, implied and expressly stated, to customers.

That means exceeding the usual expectations and going beyond the minimum corporate standard.

There are numerous instances in which Starbucks over-delivers on its promises.

One example is what Starbucks calls the Ten Minute Rule. This rule is so named because every Starbucks store opens ten minutes earlier than its hours of operation sign promises and stays open ten minutes later than its promised posted closing time. Early morning customers are appreciative of Starbucks opening its doors earlier for them, as are the night-time customers appreciative of Starbucks staying open later to satisfy their night-owl coffee cravings.

The Ten Minute Rule has become an institutionalized, minimum expectation at Starbucks—over-delivering on its promised hours of operation is now the norm. But that's just one way in which Starbucks over-delivers.

The most important part of over-delivering on promises to customers is having conscientious employees who make over-delivering a part of their everyday on-the-job way of life. (You'll learn more about hiring conscientious people with Tribal Truism #37, "Brands Are Made Possible by People.") Take the following scenario as an example: A woman enters a Starbucks with her two young, cranky children, carrying two armloads of shopping bags and looking completely overwhelmed. She finds a table and tries to corral her kids, who are about to revolt. If ever someone was in need of a rewarding everyday coffee moment, it's this young mother. Because it is later in the morning, the AM rush has died down, and the barista behind the counter is freer to roam. What does she or he do?

Hopefully, baristas take it upon themselves to come out from behind the counter and take the woman's order at her table. At the very least, they try to lighten the customer's load by not making her come up to the counter with her kids in tow. Perhaps they even upgrade her beverage order from a grande to a venti or bring out a complimentary muffin for her kids to tear into. If the employees have the disposition to think this way and have the discretion to make these kinds of small but significant decisions for themselves, they, and the company for that matter, will over-deliver every chance they can.

Who wouldn't want to be a customer of a business like that?

One Starbucks customer in Salt Lake City no doubt has been the recipient of such conscientious customer service from Starbucks—probably on numerous occasions. For a few years every year, he or she would deposit, anonymously, a $1,000 dollar bill into the tip jar during the holidays because the baristas at that particular Starbucks so over-delivered on the company's promise. (An amazingly true story that serves as a reminder Starbucks is not in the coffee business but, rather, the people business.)

Think about the best gifts you've given to other people; how often have you heard someone say, with surprised gratitude, "You didn't have to do that!" That's the essence of over-delivering on promises made. It takes people with the desire to go above and beyond what is required or expected to make that deeply personal reaction happen, and then building that culture into every part of your business.

Fulfilling promises matters. However, finding ways to over-deliver when fulfilling promises matters more, much more.

Leading Questions . . .

- In what ways, if any, does your company over-deliver on its promises to customers on a regular basis?
- What obstacles stand in the way of creating a company culture that over-delivers on promises not as the exception but more as the norm?
- What policies or programs could your company implement to over-deliver on promises?

Practice
Local Warming

Starbucks may be global in scope, but it strives to be local in function through being a good neighbor in the communities it serves. At Starbucks, being a good neighbor means actively participating in locally relevant community and charitable events. It's how Starbucks practices local warming while also practicing global growing.

To this day, as has been for many years, new Starbucks stores open in cities around the world with pre-opening charity events benefiting local nonprofits. Stores make daily donations of unsold pastries and past-date coffee to local charities. Every store functions as a local community gathering spot, whether the store is situated in an urban downtown setting, out in the suburbs, or in a rural town. Plus, Starbucks and its customers have donated upwards of 5 million books and toys to hundreds of local charities through store-driven and company-driven charity drives.

One of the reasons Starbucks dedicates time and resources to participating in these community events is that
its mission statement specifically guides the company to
contribute positively to the communities and the environment it serves. But another underlying and potentially
more important reason why Starbucks dedicates time and
resources to community events is that it helps to reduce
community "push-back" flare-ups.

It's no secret that the rapid expansion of Starbucks
has resulted in resistance from community activists wanting to keep their town free of so-called generic, global retailers. Starbucks has learned that its reputation and track
record for being a good neighbor helps to reduce many of
the community "push-back" issues paving the way for
Starbucks to open more stores within a city. (Tribal Truth
#33, "The Employee Experience Matters," highlights an
example of how Starbucks dealt with resistance in one
community and the role its employment practices played
in winning the community over.)

One important way Starbucks practices local warming is by encouraging its employees to volunteer through
its Make Your Mark program, where the company donates
dollars for each hour an employee spends volunteering at
a nonprofit organization. This program began in 2000,
and so far Starbucks employees in the United States and
Canada have contributed more than 800,000 hours of
their time helping others.

However, most companies struggle to make a business
case for community involvement. Measuring the business

impact of participating in locally relevant community and charity events beyond a feel-good measurement is just not enough. Thus, they choose not to make community involvement a business priority.

Besides helping to reduce community "push-back," Starbucks makes the business case for community participation by quantifying its impact in five ways:

1. *It increases employee morale, work performance, and attendance.* Starbucks has learned when its store-level baristas actively participate in community events, they feel better about themselves, and that, in turn, makes them more enthusiastic employees for the company.

2. *It increases employee retention rates.* Starbucks has noticed there is a correlation between store-level turnover rates and employee community participation. The more a barista volunteers in the community as a Starbucks employee, the longer the barista stays with the company.

3. *It increases employees' leadership skills.* Because Starbucks is a growing company opening up multiple stores a day, it needs new leaders to emerge in order to manage those stores. When store-level employees actively volunteer their time to charitable causes, they gain valuable leadership skills, making them more qualified to fill vacant store management positions.

4. **It enhances the company's reputation.** Community involvement improves the company's reputation as a caring, credible, and integral part of the neighborhood. By giving back and investing in the local neighborhood, companies attract good local customers—people who care about their communities—as well as the most talented and conscientious employees. Over time, a good company reputation will build trust among the public, who will be much more likely to give the company the benefit of the doubt during tough times, controversies, or scandals. By enriching the communities in which it does business, Starbucks has consistently ranked among *Fortune* magazine's "100 Best Companies to Work For" and "Ten Most Admired Companies in America," as well as *Business Ethics* magazine's "100 Best Corporate Citizens."

5. **It improves a publicly traded company's stock performance and attracts investors.** Companies with strong reputations for social responsibility enjoy an elite status among investors. According to Ronald Alsop in his book, *18 Immutable Laws of Corporate Reputation*, investors are willing to pay more for stocks of companies that have good reputations and, therefore, less perceived risk.

Starbucks' business case for community involvement extends beyond improved employee relations to improved financials. As we learned in the Tribal Truth #5

"Brand Management Is Reputation Management" lesson, Starbucks takes its reputation seriously. A positive reputation (earned, in part, through local warming) brings in new customers, attracts investors, leads to greater sales, and, ultimately, results in strong stock performance.

Though Starbucks is a major global player, it's the community connections that are keeping it in play. Local warming positively impacts the global performance of employees and the bottom line—both of which make for the best experiences possible for the customers.

Leading Questions . . .

- Is your company a valued member of the communities in which it serves?
- What is your business doing to improve the community it serves? List the ways in which your company is involved with local nonprofit groups, educational institutions, and other significant "give-back" programs or events.
- What are your company's core values? How could you give back to your community in a way that meaningfully expresses these core values?

Be Nice. Be Clean.

A staggering 40 million unique people visit Starbucks each week around the world. Of these customers, 20 percent are considered "extreme loyalists," visiting a minimum of 2 times per week, equating to over 100 visits per year. Furthermore, 8 out every 10 of these extreme loyalists' coffee purchases are made at a Starbucks.

Starbucks must have an intricate and expensive customer relationship marketing (CRM) application driving the extreme loyalty of its customers, right?

Nope.

Well, then, it must be the coffee that keeps customers coming back time and time again, right?

Not necessarily.

It may come as a surprise to you to learn the important factors in creating enthusiastically satisfied customers at Starbucks has nothing to do with CRM applications and little to do with coffee. But they have everything to do with friendly baristas and clean stores.

You'd think factors like having high-quality coffee, fast service, and appropriate prices would be the most important determinants of creating satisfied customers. But that's not the case at Starbucks. Internal Starbucks research has shown time and time again that customer loyalty at Starbucks boils down to the high-touch factors of employees being nice and stores being clean.

With that customer insight in hand, Starbucks created a ridiculously simple, yet highly effective mantra— "Be Nice. Be Clean."

For years, beginning in the late 1990s, Starbucks management preached those four words at every opportunity. And because the mantra was easy to understand and easy to act upon, it was quickly adopted and acted upon by store partners.

Starbucks has learned that *being nice* and *being clean* is the least complicated, yet most effective customer loyalty program a retailer can implement.

Leading Questions . . .

- What basic, but often overlooked, features of your company's products and/or services make the biggest impact on your customer's experience?

Touchology Trumps Technology

*If we greet customers, exchange a few words with them,
and then custom-make a drink exactly to their taste,
they will be eager to come back.*

HOWARD SCHULTZ
(Marc Gobe, Emotional Branding, p. xxxi.)

Developing a loyal customer base at Starbucks is not an overly complicated process. As Howard Schultz noted in the preceding quote, it's nothing more than greeting customers in a friendly manner and making a drink exactly to their wants.

But that seemingly simple blueprint is exactly how Starbucks cultivates a fanatically loyal customer base. The foundation for this blueprint starts with Starbucks viewing each customer interaction as a *high-touch* experience.

From the way customers are greeted by a barista to the way their handcrafted espresso beverage is ordered, prepared, and enjoyed, each customer's experience at

Starbucks is individually customer-ized through high-touch means.

Delivering great customer experiences through *touchology* requires companies to trust their employees to be themselves when connecting on a personal level with customers. Unfortunately, too many companies are reluctant to place that much trust and responsibility in the hands of employees when interacting with customers.

Instead of trusting their employees to be human, most companies attempt to replicate personal interaction through *high-teching* their business with technology. Be it loyalty cards to recognize and reward frequent customers, self-service kiosks to increase efficiency, or automated phone systems to facilitate servicing customers, these high-tech methods drive the human equation out of the business transaction.

It's not that Starbucks hasn't tried high-tech methods to improve the customer experience. Indeed, they have.

In one experiment, Starbucks sought to increase speed of service, an important factor in delivering a great customer experience, by implementing a high-tech, hand-held ordering system designed to reduce the logjam of customers ordering at the register. A store partner, with techno gadget in hand, would take orders from customers standing in line and wirelessly beam each customer's order to a barista at the espresso bar. While this high-tech ordering system did improve speed of service, customer feedback negated the efficiency gains. Customers complained that the mechanized ordering system was too impersonal and took away from their overall experience. Starbucks ditched this high-tech ordering system and went back to the high-touch method of personally connecting with customers at the register during the ordering process.

Many retailers grab onto any high-tech advancement they think will speed efficiency along at their stores, seemingly oblivious to the depersonalizing effect it may be having on its customers. Home Depot, the home improvement chain that grew so quickly in the '90s—due in large part to its renowned customer service—in 2002 instituted self-service checkout in many of its stores. So have a number of grocery stores and other retailers in the past few years. As if checking out at a home improvement or grocery store weren't impersonal enough—with the processing of the credit card now the job of the customer, after waiting in line, we're now being encouraged to scan our items, bag them, and basically do everything the clerk used to do. Presumably, we have the option of telling ourselves to "Have a nice day!" as we finish checking ourselves out. You have to wonder how deep a connection customers have with a company when they opt to avoid the checkout clerks in an attempt to get out of the store as fast as humanly possible.

While this kind of high-tech automation might be justified by some businesses, it betrays your basic mission if you're trying to create remarkable products and deliver memorable customer experiences. When automation is implemented solely for the benefit of the company's bottom

line, customers realize it. They notice the subtle, yet percep-
tible shift away from them and toward the business. And today's customer doesn't appreciate being short-changed.
They will put up with it if they have little or no choice, but
given another choice, it's not difficult to predict what they
will do.

Starbucks has embraced technology, ultimately, only
when it enhances the customer experience, making it easier to provide more rewarding everyday moments to people. If automated espresso machines can deliver the same
high-quality coffee that was previously brewed by hand,
but frees up baristas to interact more with their customers,
then that's a good thing. If it keeps the barista from being
able to talk with the person on the other side of the
counter, then what's the advantage of that?

Starbucks began experimenting with in-store CD-
burning kiosks in 2004 with its Hear Music™ Listening
Bars at select stores in Seattle and Austin. Starbucks has
since expanded this CD-burning initiative to include
Hear-Music-branded coffeehouses in Santa Monica, San
Antonio, and Miami. In extending its Hear Music business, Starbucks is hoping to add another dimension to
the in-store experience it offers. Enabling customers to
browse tunes and burn custom music CDs is definitely
high-tech, and it is also a self-service concept. How well
this concept works out is yet to be known. But Starbucks
is certain to keep its own ears open for feedback from customers and store employees. If the music kiosks and Hear
Music coffee bars enhance the experience of enjoying

coffee in stores and adds to the feeling of community and connectedness, then the technology will have aided the touchology.

But it always has to come back to the people—and ensuring that, as former Starbucks executive Howard Behar famously said, Starbucks remains "in the people business serving coffee" and not the other way around.

For Starbucks, high-touching its business is about empowering and trusting store partners to be real, to be genuine, and—by all means—to be human. Starbucks does not give partners a detailed script that instructs them what to say and how to act with customers. Instead, Starbucks acknowledges that store-level baristas have been trained to understand all facets of the business, and the company trusts these partners to show their personality when interacting with customers.

Starbucks has learned that customers appreciate the high-touch human interaction with store partners and not the high-tech mechanisms that attempt to emulate personal relationships, but are a poor substitute for the real thing.

High-touching its business through touchology is one more example of how Starbucks is in the people business serving coffee and not in the coffee business serving people.

Leading Questions . . .

- As your company has grown, in which ways has it adopted more automated systems that limit the personal interaction between you and your customers? Or that shift labor from your employees to your customers?
- What are some ways in which you can mitigate these effects, if possible, without sacrificing the added efficiency automation brings?
- How could your business better use technology and automation to increase the human touch in customer interactions?

Be Generous

"Give, and you shall receive." It's an old and overused proverb. And for good reason . . . it works. The more kindness we give others, the more kindness we receive. The more knowledge we share with others, the more knowledge we personally receive in return. The more generous we are, the more generously we profit.

This principle of generosity applies directly to Starbucks. In fact, it can be argued Starbucks' business was built on sampling generously.

To succeed, Starbucks had to change the worldview of the masses that only imagined coffee to be a hot, brown, tasteless, yet caffeinated liquid. In order to change this worldview, Starbucks had to dramatically and demonstratively alter people's understanding of what coffee should taste like, a task made even more challenging because a cup of brewed Starbucks coffee is much stronger, bolder, and more intensely flavorful than the common cup of coffee.

Starbucks accomplished this seismic worldview shift through sampling generously. For Starbucks, tasting is believing. Back when Starbucks was a small company acting big, sampling of coffees and espresso drinks was nearly omnipresent throughout the day. When you visited a Starbucks, chances were, there would be a taster-cup sample of a just-made drink ready for the tasting. Sampling became ingrained as part of the Starbucks business culture as the more customers tasted, the more they believed that coffee should taste just like that.

Tasting is more than believing at Starbucks, it's also sales-driving. Internal company studies have revealed for every five beverages Starbucks samples to customers, it triggers a purchase (an impressive 20-percent-conversion rate).

When Starbucks launches a new beverage, the most effective sales-driving tool is not advertising it on the radio, it's sampling it directly to customers.

The same goes for when Starbucks wants to drive sales of whole bean coffees; it doesn't advertise. Instead, the company's generous sampling of coffee to its in-store customers ultimately drives sales for whole bean coffee.

One of the most successful sampling initiatives at Starbucks has been its "Chill Patrol," which brings Frappuccino blended beverages to people at planned and unplanned community events during the warm summer months. Using a Volkswagen van, retrofitted to essentially be a mobile store, the Chill Patrol goes to sponsored charity events and shows up on the spur of the moment to surprise and delight people at local little league baseball games or other community activities. They sample Frappuccinos and sometimes sell them to people who just can't get enough Starbucks. The promotion builds terrific goodwill and positive word-of-mouth. In addition, according to internal studies, the Chill Patrol marketing activity delivers a significantly high return on investment compared to more traditional marketing tactics.

Successful companies such as Whole Foods, Great Harvest Bread Company, and Trader Joe's also use generous sampling of their products to drive sales. But doing this does more than drive sales on specific products—it's a long-term strategy for converting customers into loyal followers.

Everybody loves getting stuff for free. But this sampling notion goes beyond the simple concept of giving customers a little something for nothing. Sampling should be and, at Starbucks, is an act of pride and not simply a device to increase sales. Because sampling solely to *sell* is devoid of genuine pride in a product or service, customers sense this and will shy away from the shill. Sampling to *share* personifies your appreciation and pride in your product, which customers also understand and will become more enthusiastic and eager to buy. Giving away free samples powerfully demonstrates to consumers the pride you have in your products. This pride breeds trust—there's nothing underhanded or suspect about it. Your customers are smart enough to realize you're offering them food and drink samples because you hope they'll love it. They're hoping to find that great product that fulfills their desire. By giving it away, you're showing customers how sure you are they'll love it and want it again and again.

When Starbucks samples, it's telling its customers, "Hey, we're not just going to tell you how great our new beverage is (that would be out-right advertising), we're going to prove it to you. Try it yourself, on us."

The other important thing this kind of sampling does is transform the chain coffeehouse, or chain anything, into more of the small, local shop run by proud people you want to get to know. People have come to expect certain kinds of behavior from chains—consistency, convenience, mediocre quality, low prices, and the impersonal vibe you get from a large, faceless corporation. When you put a face on the corporation, it ceases to feel like a "chain." When you turn a multi-unit business into a mom-and-pop store, you've become part of the fabric of the neighborhood. When you offer samples of gourmet beverages as if you were a tiny Sonoma Valley winery, you've become a destination—no matter how ubiquitous you may appear.

As important as it is to sample, it's just as critical to think about *how* you sample. How much focus do you put on it? Do people who walk into the store—both long-time customers and first-timers—recognize there's something new or special to sample, and that you're excited about turning them on to it? Does it feel like you're trying to force it on them (the sampling equivalent of "You want fries with that?") or inviting them to partake in a comfortable, friendly way? The way you present the sample, the placement in store, the time of day it's offered, the way the person explains the new product to customers—all of these things matter and play a role in driving new product sales and building personal connections with customers.

Perhaps the most critical factor in how you sample is whether it's passive or active. Customers experience two types of sampling at Starbucks—passive sampling and active sampling. *Passive sampling* happens when customers help themselves to a product sample that is sitting on a table or near the main register. *Active sampling* occurs when a store partner serves samples to customers and engages them in conversation. Active sampling is by far the best way to connect with customers and drive sales.

And that was the motivation for Blended Beverage BINGO, a behind-the-scenes promotion Starbucks ran in the summer of 2001. Seeking to create a store-level incentive contest to goose sales of its blended beverages, former long-time Starbucks marketer Paul Williams and I put our heads together and brainstormed for a creative and unconventional solution. We recognized how critical sampling had always been to product sales success and to Starbucks' success in general, and we tried to think of something that would encourage baristas to engage in active sampling and interact with customers as much as possible. For some reason, we started talking about board games—the kind we had all played as kids, like LIFE, Sorry!, Mousetrap—and toyed with the idea of turning the incentive contest into a board game. Because one of us had played BINGO the night before, we decided that we should make our contest a version of BINGO, but substitute activities for numbers. The activities would be different ways for baristas to engage customers, for example: sample a Mocha Frappuccino to a customer working on a laptop; or sample a Tazoberry to a customer wearing a red article of clothing; or, in the case of one really wacky center-square activity, we asked the baristas to get five customers and two partners to form an in-store conga line.

Not only was this program fun for store partners, it was fun for customers. One store sent the Starbucks marketing team its completed BINGO board and a laminated poster featuring photos of store partners and customers doing all 25 activities on the BINGO card.

Blended Beverage BINGO has been widely credited as a hallmark customer-interaction program that is still talked about today at Starbucks as an example of a great customer experience program. It accomplished a number of objectives in several ways—driving sales and building on the sense of community between Starbucks, its employees, and its customers—but first and foremost, it created a fun, interesting way to reward our customers, while enhancing the Starbucks culture of generously sampling.

To drive sales and transform customers into devoted followers, follow the "sample example" not the advertising example, show the pride you have in your product, share it, and be generous.

Leading Questions . . .

- Do you have the pride in your products and/or services that if you gave samples away, your customers would beat a path to your door demanding more?
- If you are sampling, or are planning to, how will you do it to ensure it is effective? fun? memorable?

Future Success Stems from Past Success

What's truly impressive about the remarkable sales growth at Starbucks is that it's been achieved organically and not artificially. In other words, sales growth has come from maintaining and further deepening its connection with existing customers and not from artificially trying to drive sales through acquiring new customers in new markets with new brands.

Starbucks achieves organic sales through opening more locations, improving the efficiency of store operations, and introducing new (more expensive) coffee beverages. By focusing on growth opportunities close to its comfortable home of coffee, Starbucks achieves sustainable sales growth that makes any retailer envious.

However, while sales growth has come relatively easy to Starbucks, the company has had to overcome the occasional, and at times substantial, bump in the road in achieving sustainable sales growth.

The first bump came in the mid-to-late '90s, when Starbucks' upper management was convinced that once the company reached 10,000 North American locations, the coffee market would be saturated and growth prospects would be at a standstill (which, as it turns out, was a false premonition). As a result, Starbucks began to aggressively pursue growth opportunities by extending its core business. The company ramped up international expansion and increased its whole bean distribution in grocery stores. Both of these efforts successfully leveraged Starbucks' core competency in coffee to grow the overall business.

The second bump in the road to sustainable sales growth came in 1999, when Starbucks, still concerned its future growth prospects were slowing, decided to seek growth in areas outside of its comfortable home of coffee. The prevailing wisdom of Starbucks' upper management guiding this growth strategy was: "Our customers have given us permission to branch out into lifestyle areas beyond coffee."

Seeking future sales success through branching out into lifestyle areas beyond coffee had Starbucks going into ventures such as

- an aggressive and expensive plan to morph the Starbucks.com Web site into an Internet lifestyle portal offering consumers everything from kitchen appliances to living room furniture;

- opening Starbucks Cafés, full-scale restaurants fea-turing home-style comfort food;
- publishing *Joe*, a hip literary culture magazine; and
- focusing its in-store merchandise on lifestyle prod-ucts such as pencil sharpeners, leather bound jour-nals, desk clocks, and other decorative office accessories.

Each of these lifestyle brand growth ventures failed. The permission Starbucks believed its customers had granted them turned out to be a marketing mirage—no visible customers and no visible market.

Following these failed forays into lifestyle brand exten-sions, the prevailing wisdom of Starbucks' upper manage-ment became: "Sometimes you have to leave home to realize how sweet home really is." Thus, Starbucks pledged to seek sales growth opportunities by focusing supremely on areas closer to home—its core business of coffee.

These days, Starbucks is generating organic growth by staying closer to its home of coffee. It's sticking to its roots but taking a new look at old assumptions. Starbucks previously didn't think there was a market for specialty coffee in small towns scattered throughout the United States. Now that the word (and the Starbucks coffee habit) has spread to these smaller cities, Starbucks is ded-icating a significant portion of its new store growth to opening locations in American cities with populations less than 100,000.

The company is expanding in other coffee-centered ways as well: opening more locations throughout the world, introducing new coffee beverages, and finding new ways to enhance the in-store coffee experience through offering customers the convenience of using a prepaid debit card, known as the Starbucks Card, and by making its stores hot spots for wireless Internet (wi-fi) connectivity.

With Starbucks now believing the global coffee market will hold a minimum of 30,000 Starbuck locations, the prospects are bright that the company will continue to achieve future sales success by focusing on its core competency of delivering great coffee and great coffee experiences.

Even with its current success and growth, Starbucks is once again being enticed to seek sales growth in areas far outside its comfortable home of coffee. While it's been successful in merchandising music in recent years, the company is dedicating significant resources to producing and selling CDs under its Hear Music record label and to installing music CD-burning kiosks in its stores.

Its most recent promotion involved a marketing tie-in with the independent film, *Akeelah and the Bee*, about an African-American girl who enters the National Spelling Bee. The film correlated well with the diverse lifestyles and aspirational attitudes of Starbucks customers, and Howard Schultz believed they would welcome the movie's message and promotion in stores. "We've experienced great success with the music we offer in our stores," Howard said, "and we recognized that we had an opportunity to extend the trust our customers have in the Starbucks brand to bring them other forms of entertainment."

Time will tell if focusing on music retailing and other forms of entertainment marketing will have Starbucks regretting its decision to leave its comfortable home of coffee in search of new ways to grow sales. Starbucks may be wise to heed its own tribal knowledge advice of "future success stems from past success" and focus more on coffee and less on music and movies to grow the business.

Leading Questions . . .

- List the ways your business has potentially left "home" in search of sales?
- If you feel your business is lost being away from "home," what must change in order to course correct your business to get "back home" again?

Tourists Bring Home Souvenirs. Explorers Bring Home Stories.

Starbucks marketers treat customers not as occasional tourists seeking superficial trinkets but as everyday explorers seeking stories.

Everyday explorers crave authentic experiences, big or small, that will enhance their social lives. Each Starbucks location serves as a community town hall where people gather as a group or as individuals to experience life in their own ways. Starbucks simply provides a comfortable space and social lubricants (coffee drinks), enabling people to share old stories or create new stories with each other or with themselves.

Starbucks marketers have outlined five ways in which customers experience Starbucks. One way is as part of a ritualistic morning routine. A second way is as a meeting place with friends and family. Then there are the professionals who use Starbucks as an appropriate and comfortable place to socialize around business dealings. Customers also use Starbucks as a treat occasion where they will reward themselves with a decadently tasty beverage. The fifth way customers experience Starbucks is as a place to retreat from all the excesses in life and just take a moment to exhale.

In many ways, the experience of enjoying coffee with others has become more important to Starbucks than the coffee itself. Starbucks marketers know experiences provide customers with rich and compelling stories to share with others, while products typically satiate immediate, basic needs.

When companies view customers as explorers, they create rich, multidimensional experiences that go beyond superficial sightseeing to lifestyle immersion. Tourists are satisfied with the dime tour. Explorers demand more. They do not want to be shortchanged on their visit. Mental images are more meaningful than tourist snapshots. Explorers are eager to learn, they want to linger in an area and soak up the atmosphere. Explorers want to immerse themselves in the area, while the tourists want only what they see on the travel posters. Tourists want to bring home a T-shirt from their travels; explorers want to bring home an experience.

Treating customers as explorers and not just quick, in-and-out tourists means that the company has to go above and beyond. While that may take more physical and fiscal efforts, the payoff (in customer loyalty and in revenue) is worth it. The financial rewards to Starbucks in treating its customers as explorers are significant as company research clearly indicates customers buy more the longer they linger at Starbucks.

But the challenge Starbucks has in appealing to everyday explorers is going beyond meeting their every day needs to meeting their ever-increasing wants. These smart and savvy customers have high expectations and make conscientious buying decisions every day with every dollar they spend. They are tired of the hucksterism that comes with the incessant hawking of unremarkable products from most retailers. And they seek to be interesting and interested.

Everything about the Starbucks experience is designed to be interesting to get everyday explorers interested, interested enough to share their Starbucks stories with friends and family.

Leading Questions . . .

- How might customers view your company as the equivalent of a business "tourist trap"?
- What part of your business have you allowed your customers to explore? What experiences could you offer your customers so that they'd return wanting to learn and see more?

Foster Customer Devotion

We're not in the coffee business serving people.
We're in the people business serving coffee.

HOWARD BEHAR,
former Starbucks executive

Starbucks has fostered loyalty beyond reason with its customers. Many Starbucks customers are lovingly devoted to Starbucks the business and Starbucks the brand. To foster customer loyalty that borders on customer devotion, Starbucks follows an unwritten but business-innate marketing mindset of enriching a customer's life, not entrapping it.

Most marketing activities from companies seeking to build customer loyalty are designed more to capture customers than to captivate customers. "Preferred Shopper" cards from supermarkets, frequent flier miles from airlines, and lengthy service agreements from cellular companies all entrap us into being labeled "loyal customers" by companies.

Most times, these customer-loyalty schemes are based upon offering customers lower prices to gain greater loyalty. But loyalty isn't earned by offering the lowest price. Businesses that gain sales solely by pricing low are only as good as their latest, cheapest offer. As soon as a competitor can beat the price, all those "loyal" customers will chuck their cards and shop elsewhere.

These "Preferred Shopper" promotions also reverse the logic of great customer service: They ask customers to sign up for a card or buy a certain amount of product before they can enjoy the benefits of being part of the club. Do you really want to create two classes of customers? One that gets the "good stuff" at a good price, the other that gets a raw deal? If you want to foster true customer devotion, don't make your customers jump through hoops just to feel welcome, or "preferred."

Businesses operating like this treat their customers like cattle, doing whatever they can to attract attention. When companies are more focused on their own bottom line than their customers, both will eventually fall away. These programs lack soul and meaning to stand the test of time.

Starbucks seeks to captivate (not capture) and enrich (not entrap) the lives of its customers through rewarding everyday moments. The company understands a great coffee moment can provide customers with hope, inspiration, and connectivity. A Starbucks coffee moment offers customers a semblance of hope in their cluttered lives. Many of Starbucks' most devoted customers seek refuge from their workplace, their home life, and the daily commute in-between. To these customers, Starbucks is a place where they can go to regroup, reconnect, recharge, and rest.

Coffee has been the fuel for creativity and inspiration since the 16th century. And in the 21st century, Starbucks provides customers with a modern-day place where their souls can be nurtured and inspired on a daily basis.

But the real customer devotional magic of Starbucks resides in the magic of how coffee connects. Coffee connects as no other beverage does. It connects the morning to the night as many customers begin their day with a cup of Starbucks and end their day with a cup of decaf from the same store. Coffee connects people with people, as many friendships begin and are continuously nurtured over coffee. And just as important, a cup coffee enjoyed in solitude can connect one with oneself.

Customer loyalty works both ways, and Starbucks knows that. Of course Starbucks wants to maintain its profitability, but it does this by helping the folks who come into its stores, not by working against them. If you want customers to stay loyal to you, stay loyal to your customers—treat them as people, help them as individuals, offer them something extra, and they'll come back for more.

BRAND LOYALTY MATRIMONY

Is there a brand you feel so strongly about—from a value relationship and an emotional relationship—you would declare your unconditional loyalty to?

Is there a brand you would marry?

As in all good relationships, fostering customer devotion and brand loyalty is a two-way street. It starts with what your brand has to offer. If you provide a remarkable experience, the rewards are profound and long-lasting.

Below is a tongue-in-cheek set of marriage vows, joining together a devoted customer with a faithful brand.

Brand Loyalty Matrimony Ceremony

We are gathered here today to unite this customer, *[insert Customer name]*, with this brand, *[insert Brand name]*, in the bonds of a true reciprocal relationship known as brand loyalty matrimony.

If any competing brand or any customer evangelist can show just cause why these two should not be joined, then let them speak now or forever lose the business opportunity.

[Customer name], will you take this brand as your partner to engage in commerce with in the holy estate of brand loyalty matrimony?

Will you evangelize her, respect her, provide customer feedback to her in good experiences and in bad experiences; forsaking all others, be true to her as long as you both shall live? (I will.)

[Brand name], will you take this customer as your partner to engage in commerce with in the holy estate of brand loyalty matrimony? Will you respect him, deliver upon all promises to him, be truthful to him and reward him with the highest quality goods or services and the best customer service in good economic times and in bad economic times as long as you both shall live? (I will.)

Please join hands and repeat after me (customer first).

I, *[Customer name]*, take *[Brand name]*, as my loyal brand of choice to buy from and to evangelize for from this day forward until bankruptcy do us part.

I, *[Brand name]*, take *[Customer name]*, as a loyal customer to help them actualize their aspirations and to deliver the greatest value to from this day forward until bankruptcy do us part.

By the authority vested in me from the *Lovemarks* writings of Kevin Roberts, I pronounce this consumer and this brand to be loyal to one another.

You may now kiss the competitors good-bye.

Leading Questions . . .

- How many companies are you devoted to? What do they offer above other like-minded competitors? How do they treat you differently?
- Does your company respect its customers in spite of the bottom-line profitability pressures? How does it show its loyalty to the customers?
- Does your company captivate its customer's devotion beyond offering low prices? If so, do you think those customers know the meaningful differences between your company and its closest competitor?

Walls Talk.
Take a Moment to Listen.

Legend has it that Howard Behar, a long-time and now-retired Starbucks executive, could walk into a Starbucks, pause for a moment, and then gauge a store's profitability and its employee morale on the spot.

Forget scouring over a store's profit and loss (P&L) report or reviewing employee surveys, HB, as Howard Behar is known within the Starbucks tribe, could gauge a store's profitability and employee morale just by listening to what the walls were telling him. You may wonder, what were the walls actually telling him? How did they speak?

The walls talk through sounds and sights, words and music, and energy. A store with a positive vibe will have customers using the tables to chat with one another, to read, and to work. The expressions on the faces of the customers and the employees will be bright and calm; the tone of voice of the people talking will be friendly, warm, laughing. One of those customers may, in fact, be an off-the-clock employee who feels so comfortable in the store it's where he chooses to spend his free time, as well. The floors are clean, the baristas are cheerful to the customers and to one another. Overall, it's a pleasant and relaxing place to be. HB knew that a Starbucks that created this kind of environment was usually more profitable and had lower employee turnover rates.

On the other side, a Starbucks with a bad vibe—muttering, disgruntled walls—will have customers coming in to get coffee and leaving right away. It is usually struggling financially and has a difficult time keeping a full, energetic staff. Customers and employees of a store feed off the store's energy, and the store's energy—the walls—feeds off that of the customers and employees.

HB made his observations on the Starbucks business by observing the business firsthand. By sitting in the store and acting as a customer, he could take new eyes (and ears) to the surroundings. Behar encouraged Starbucks baristas and managers to view their own stores from the perspective of a customer as well. Store managers who can "hear" the walls—those who are conscientious of the look and feel of the store and who work hard to keep the vibe positive—usually are first in line to take over a "high-potential" location that is suffering. Besides running a profitable store, successful and observant managers will be rewarded with the responsibility to manage higher-profile stores, based on the positive vibes of the stores they've previously managed.

All walls talk, no matter the business. Walls say something good or bad about businesses every day. The problem is, many businesspeople do not spend enough time in their stores to know what the walls are telling them. Instead they rely on second-hand reports or scrutinize store-specific financials to make observations. The solution is as easy as sitting in the store and observing. Keep in mind, if you can hear what the walls are telling you, your customers certainly can.

Leading Questions . . .

- Put yourself in the shoes of an outsider. Pretend to be a customer in your own store or office. How are customers interacting with one another and with employees? What does the atmosphere feel like? Are you feeling positive or negative vibes? What are your walls telling you?

Access Alters How a Business Achieves Success

[Starbucks is] always managing the tension between opposites.
On the one hand, I'd say we're comforting and predictable,
yet on the other hand, we're constantly surprising and delighting.

DEIDRA WAGER,
former Starbucks executive
(internal Starbucks presentation, Seattle, WA)

Starbucks will not deny it is everywhere. But it is everywhere because customers want Starbucks to be everywhere. Otherwise, they wouldn't be there. (Starbucks is smart like that.)

Starbucks works under the premise of being everywhere customers want them to be. And, according to internal research studies, customers would be more satisfied if they had a Starbucks more convenient to them. So Starbucks satisfies customers by opening more stores in more places to be more convenient to more people.

People no longer have to go out of their way to find a Starbucks. Starbucks, instead, must go out of its way—by showing up seemingly everywhere—to find and satisfy customers. It is startling to note Starbucks is fast approaching having one store for every 10,000 people living in cities like Seattle, Atlanta, Dallas, Boston, and Oakland. Yet, Starbucks' excess access is not impeding financial success. Since going public in 1992, year-over-year sales growth at Starbucks has exceeded 5 percent or better—that's 14 consecutive years of extremely healthy sales.

Starbucks can afford to keep opening new stores— yes, sometimes even across the street from one another— because it keeps a close eye on a store's capacity and the scope of potential customers in a specific area. If a store is seen at being close to maximum capacity, that is the store is running full throttle, the company will look at opening another one in the area—one that will attract new customer traffic and take some of the pressure off the existing store. While the old store will take a hit—it will probably see a sales decline of 15 percent—customers will be pleased with the shorter lines, less frazzled baristas, and a more open, calming environment.

The sheer number of store locations, however, has changed Starbucks' business proposition. Starbucks no longer can compete on being quirky and quaint. Let's face it: It's hard to be unique when you're opening five new stores a day. Instead, Starbucks competes on being consistent and convenient. That perfect shot of espresso that Starbucks used to grow its customer base back in the '90s now has to be the same perfect shot every time that a customer walks into the store, whether the store is in St. Louis or Shanghai. Consistency is paramount at this scale, meaning that everything in the store has to be modularized. In such a plug-and-play environment, it is possible to plug some quaintness into the stores—like customizing the atmosphere to match the local culture—but, now, consistency and convenience come first.

Of course, this strategy presents an opportunity for a challenger brand to step up and recreate the quirky side of the specialty coffee industry. Because the type of employees and customers who gravitate toward quaint and quirky often tend to support an underdog, such a challenger could generate worthy competition. For Starbucks, though, exchanging unique sensibilities for consistency and convenience keeps a competitive edge. Ultimately, it has been a trade-off that satisfies more customers and leads to greater sales success.

Leading Questions . . .

- What sacrifices is your company willing to make to satisfy your customers?
- How does consistency and convenience work into your company's overall game plan? Are these qualities prioritized?

Everything Matters

*We had a mission, to educate consumers everywhere
about fine coffee. We had a vision, to create an atmosphere in our
stores that drew people in and gave them a sense of wonder and
romance in the midst of their harried lives. We had an idealistic
dream, that our company could be far more than the paradigm
defined by corporate America in the past.*

HOWARD SCHULTZ
(Pour Your Heart Into It)

Starbucks is an experiential brand that strives to be interesting in order to get customers interested. Because the customer experience at Starbucks is the marketing for Starbucks, everything matters.

Not just one thing . . . E-V-E-R-Y-T-H-I-N-G.

Everything matters because everything is an act of communication with customers. And E-V-E-R-Y-T-H-I-N-G includes the following:

- The package design of whole bean coffees matters.

- The hours of operation signs on the front door matters.
- The way the chocolate-covered espresso beans are merchandised on the shelves matters.
- The music playing in-store matters.
- The way baristas dress matters.
- The way your espresso drink is prepared and delivered matters.
- The promotional sign placed at the main cash register matters.
- The lighting in the restrooms matters.

E-V-E-R-Y-T-H-I-N-G to Starbucks matters.

You'd be hard pressed to find a Starbucks employee say, "That doesn't matter. No customer will ever notice it." Because chances are a customer will notice. And that's why EVERYTHING MATTERS to Starbucks.

Leading Questions . . .

- How does your company communicate to its employees and customers that everything matters? Is it apparent from the products, services, and experience you provide to customers that you embrace this ideal?
- When customers bring up problems, what kind of things do they bring up? How does your company respond?

TRE

More Tribal Truths

Creating the Kind of Workplace You'd Like to Work In

Make the Company Something to Believe In

The best internal culture a company could hope for is one where the employees are so loyal they spread word of the company and its product with fierce passion, a culture where employees go way beyond being minions to being missionaries.

Turning minions into missionaries can only happen if the employees truly believe in the company. The company with missionary employees is one where the workforce is there because it wants to be, not because it needs to be. These employees talk about the quality of the company itself, the values the company endorses, the way in which their lives are enhanced because of it.

They aren't towing the company line because there is no "line" to tow. And they certainly aren't drinking the company Kool-Aid—a concept that is derived from the horrific massacre of the Jonestown residents in the 1970s. Today, drinking the company Kool-Aid means to succumb to corporate brainwashing, to follow management's decisions without question, regardless of whether the decisions are right for the employee or the company. The problem with company Kool-Aid, so to speak, is not that it's not delicious—most often it is, padded with sweet perks to keep employees contented—but that it's poisonous. Employees who sip this dangerous cocktail of corporate culture simply mimic the corporate environment without ever considering the end result. They follow blindly to keep their benefits, not because they truly and sincerely care about the business and its impact on others.

For Starbucks, though, supportive employees aren't following blindly at all, they are choosing to follow because they are engaged in what the company is doing. They believe.

Starbucks employees have stayed passionate about the company because the company has stayed passionate about them. The company has its employees bleeding Starbucks green because it trusts and respects them. As Howard Schultz writes, "If people relate to the company they work for, if they form an emotional tie to it and buy into its dreams, they will pour their heart into making it better. When employees have self-esteem and self-respect they can contribute so much more: to their company, to their family, to the world." Starbucks sees the potential and the talent in its employees, and it wants them to see the same in themselves.

So many companies foster an atmosphere of blind followership, essentially raising puppets instead of growing employees. It's dangerous and reckless business behavior to have a workforce that merely mimics the company mission statement. Companies that foster a culture where employees are conditioned to follow blindly end up with workers whom are either willing to say and do whatever is needed to get ahead, or those who are just biding their time until the next paycheck arrives.

Starbucks employees, instead, see their company not as a means to an end but as a means to a win—a good life. They are choosing to spend their time working for and extolling the virtues of their company because they believe it's making a worthwhile contribution—that the time they spend at work makes a meaningful difference.

Strong company loyalty up and down the ranks works well for Starbucks. As long as employees have willingly signed up to work for a company they want to support, why not put that enthusiasm to use? The Starbucks company culture encourages employees to think for themselves and respond on their own volition and discretion to please customers. Because employees are free to act on their own, they freely (and willingly) act to serve customers and the company beyond the status quo.

While the company has been on an unrelenting growth pace, the employee company culture has remained relatively pure in its purpose and meaning. This culture has remained pure because of three important factors: a shared vision/shared fate, a thriving employee community, and a hire right/fire fast mentality.

SHARED VISION/SHARED FATE

Starbucks instills a shared vision among all employees of wanting to change the way the world drinks, appreciates, and experiences coffee. For store-level employees, this is done through more than 20 hours of training. In fact, one training course focuses solely on explaining what the "Starbucks Experience" is and why it is meaningful. Besides learning about the roots of the company's beginnings, new employees also learn about the rich cultural legacy of coffee. This introduction to the creation and vision of Starbucks indoctrinates each employee into the Starbucks tribe. It's here that the oral tradition, for new hires, begins.

This shared vision manifests itself in the form of shared fate and shared experiences. Starbucks believes its success is dependent upon the shared fate of all partners, corporate and store level.

THRIVING EMPLOYEE COMMUNITY

Starbucks partners are a like-minded group in that they are all passionate overachievers. More than that, Starbucks partners generally enjoy being around each other while on (and off) the job.

Starbucks encourages its partners to form working communities through cross-functional teaming. Because every department is dependent upon one another to create and implement programs, this interdependence fosters a greater feeling of community at work.

For example, during my time at Starbucks (and I'm sure to this day), the project teams the marketing department led always included a diverse group of stakeholders, from legal to supply chain to operations to creative services to store development to information technology (IT). All work at Starbucks is project work. Every job, even the seemingly easy job of filling out the paperwork needed to send marketing materials to stores, is project work. With a nod to Tom Peters, Starbucks marketers live in the projects.[1] Because every project worked on is a chance to "wow," and because every team member truly wants the same thing—company success—the element of community carries each project to completion.

HIRE RIGHT. FIRE FAST.

Starbucks believes if you hire the right person, that person will in turn, hire the right people. But sometimes, the right person will hire some wrong people. And generally speaking, Starbucks is slow to hire the "right" people but fast to fire the "wrong" people.

The "wrong" people at Starbucks have an apathetic attitude and do not believe in what the company is trying to do. These people view work as work and have no connections to the company's mission, its other employees, or even its customers. Starbucks is quick to eject apathetic employees because apathy spreads like a virus. Apathy is the enemy at Starbucks. If apathetic employees are not ejected quickly, they can cause significant harm by infecting others around them with their lackadaisical demeanor.

The right people, on the other hand, have a passion for the company and for the product. This is especially seen in those who already share the company vision before they're even hired. One of the litmus tests in the store-level hiring procedure is to offer applicants a cup of coffee during the interview. If potential employees shrug off the offer with a "No, thanks," (which, by the way, many do) how could they possibly convey enthusiasm for the store's product? How could they share a love for great coffee if they don't sip some while being interviewed for a job *in a coffee shop?* But those who do transform that first sip into a job—whether it lasts for the summer or for a career—are given a chance to find a home in the company. These people want to help customers have a positive, relaxing experience. They want to spread the word about great coffee, and they actively believe that an appreciation of good coffee actually enriches people's lives. They live the company's mission and want to succeed based on that.

Missionary employees will go above and beyond to stay true to their company, but they have to have the support of the company behind them. They must have something to believe in.

Leading Questions . . .

- Honestly, how does your company view its employees? as missionaries or minions?
- List the ways in which your company encourages, or potentially discourages, its employees to be missionaries.
- What types of shared visions and experiences do your employees have? How do those elements help to bond your employees?

The Employee Experience Matters

The best minute I spend is the one I invest in people.

HOWARD BEHAR,
former Starbucks executive
(internal Starbucks presentation)

Starbucks recognizes competitors can replicate products, but they can't replicate people. That's precisely why the company focuses so much attention on the employee experience, because it is employees who create meaningful connections with customers. Many marketers view employee relations as a job solely for human resources—they see employees as tools. But employees—happy, rewarded employees—can work wonders for the company's marketing efforts. There is no better spokesperson for a company, product, and brand than someone who is happy with his job and respected by his employer and peers. A happy employee will in turn, make customers happy.

Starbucks knows that it needs its people—from the barista-level up to the top—to be happy in their jobs for the company to succeed. The Starbucks' employee experience revolves around the "What's In It For Me" (WIIFM) factor. Pronounced "Wif-Um," this employee-first mindset is rooted deep within the culture of Starbucks: so deep, in fact, employees at Starbucks are called "partners," not "employees." The title of "partner" is also a literal one: Each employee has a direct stake in the company through stock options. Howard Schultz began the stock program, called "Bean Stock," in 1991, one year before the company went public. Each employee, full-time and part-time, is given stock options worth a percentage of his or her base pay. Because the value of the shares is tied to company profits, it's in each employees' interest that the company succeed—a win-win for company and employee.

But beyond *needing* to have happy employees, Starbucks knows its employees *deserve* to be happy. From the beginning, Howard Schultz has believed good things come when you care more for your employees more than others think you should. His decision to offer health benefits to all employees was revolutionary in the late 1980s and is still relatively unique today, especially in the food industry.

In his book *A New Brand World*, former Starbucks executive Scott Bedbury tells of a time in 1995 when he traveled to Berkeley, California, to respond to community leaders who were protesting the opening of a Starbucks. Seeing Starbucks as just another chain—another proponent of the United States of Generica—these town leaders had invited the media to their demonstration. With the belief in the Starbucks employee experience, though, Bedbury was able to turn the tables. He asked the community why they would prefer to force out a business that was willing to pay part-time employees full benefits for the local businesses that didn't offer any such employee rewards. One journalist then turned his attention to a local shop owner who was, under questioning, forced to admit he didn't pay benefits to part-timers. Starbucks went on to open that store in Berkeley and many, many more since.

In a business where the front-line employees represent the face of the company—where every transaction counts—it only makes sense to treat the store-level employees with the same respect (and benefits) as those in upper management. So while other companies, like those in the fast-food industry, put exorbitant amounts of money into marketing slogans, signage, and songs, Starbucks is putting it's money where its loyalty is—in its people. In 2004, the company spent nearly $70 million on partner recruitment and development programs. The $70 million spent on the recruiting and training of store partners is more money than Starbucks spent acquiring new customers through advertising in 2004.[1]

The WIIFM extends to the feeling of being a part of something bigger than just working for a coffee company as Starbucks is driven to change the way the world drinks and appreciates coffee.

The combination of great benefits, mutual respect, and internal bonding is the reason why so many of Starbucks' partners have stayed in the company, working their way from store barista into corporate management roles. Even more remarkable is the retention rate at the store level. While other quick service restaurants contend with employee turnover rates close to 300 percent, Starbucks is rewarded with an employee turnover rate around 65 percent. To bring those numbers to life, the typical Starbucks will change over its staff once every 18 months compared to other fast food places that will turn over staff 3 times in 12 months. This is especially significant because the barista employee pool is filled with a preponderance of 18-year-olds to 24-year-olds in a transitory life stage.

There is a reason employees want to stay at Starbucks: They are treated well. Because Starbucks realizes the employee experience matters, the company is rewarded by being viewed as an employer of choice through recognition by *Fortune* magazine as one of the "Top 100 Companies to Work For" in America since 1998. But ultimately, it is the recognition from the employees who stay and please its customers that really makes the difference. Without showing that employees matter, without treating its people better than others would expect, Starbucks would not be the company it is today.

Leading Questions . . .

- List the WIIFMs your company provides. How many of these are available only to full-time employees and not part-timers?
- Compare the turnover rates of employees in management with those at the store/customer level. How might you tighten this turnover gap discrepancy?
- Does your company place more financial emphasis on advertising than employee training? Is this consistent with your company's mission?

Live Your Mission (Statement)

We have the opportunity to build a great company,
and we intend to do it our way.
That means no matter how rapidly we grow, we'll hold fast
to the core values that made Starbucks the success it is.

STARBUCKS ANNUAL REPORT, 1996

Most mission statements read virtually the same. It seems all businesses seek to "synergistically leverage resources to exceed customer expectations while adhering to the highest industry standards and maximizing alliances to increase profitability."

There's nothing new there.

Because most mission statements are written using a never-ending stream of vacuous business clichés and positioning platitudes with no real actionable meaning, employees pay little to no attention to them. These well-intended and highly crafted expositions simply collect dust on the walls at company headquarters, only to resurface once-a-decade at "kumbaya" executive off-site meetings.

That said, would it surprise you to learn many Starbucks partners can recite, word-for-word, the Starbucks' mission statement?

Would it surprise you further to learn Starbucks receives over 200 letters a month from concerned employees questioning whether or not the company is living its mission statement?

It shouldn't. That's because the Starbucks mission statement is understandable, aspirational, and most importantly, it's actionable. It's less a statement of Starbucks' mission and more a collection of statements on how Starbucks measures the appropriateness of the business decisions they make every day in its conference rooms and stores.

Starbucks believes the real purpose of its mission statement is to help make the best, most appropriate business decisions. That's why Starbucks lists six highly actionable principles in its mission statement. Go ahead, read (and understand) for yourself . . .

Starbucks makes its mission statement a living document through encouraging all partners to question any activity they believe the company is doing that goes against company values. This process is called *Mission Review,* and each month around 200 submissions are received by Starbucks from interested and concerned employees. Every submission gets a response, many of which get more than that. They get action. This not

THE STARBUCKS MISSION STATEMENT

Establish Starbucks as the premier purveyor of the finest coffee in the world while maintaining our uncompromising principles as we grow.

The following six guiding principles will help us [Starbucks] measure the appropriateness of our decisions:

1. Provide a great work environment and treat each other with respect and dignity.
2. Embrace diversity as an essential component in the way we do business.
3. Apply the highest standards of excellence to the purchasing, roasting, and fresh delivery of our coffee.
4. Develop enthusiastically satisfied customers all of the time.
5. Contribute positively to our communities and our environment.
6. Recognize that profitability is essential to our future success.

(Source: *www.starbucks.com/aboutus/environment.asp*)

only gives each employee a voice in the company, but it keeps the company on track and in line with its original values. It lets employees know the company is listening *and* reacting to them. And, should the company implement something that was suggested, credit is given to that specific person.

For example, when Starbucks partners were called into military action following the 9/11 tragedy, Starbucks received Mission Review inquiries asking to extend its military-reserve policy to protect salaries, benefits, and employment positions for affected partners. Starbucks listened to the Mission Review submissions and responded by expanding its military reserve policy to meet the needs of its employees. The same can be said for the tuition reimbursement program. Because so many store-level employees are college-aged, the company received many Mission Review inquiries asking for such a program. The company listened and responded to these requests as well, implementing tuition reimbursement for employees with at least one-year tenure.

This Mission Review process—asking for feedback from within and working to please employees first—keeps Starbucks acting in an upstart, small-company, compassionate way, despite its now global reach. Even though it has more than 125,000 employees worldwide, Starbucks makes sure they each have a say in the direction of the company. (For more ideas on how large businesses can improve by acting smaller, see Tribal Truth #17 "A Goliath Can Become a David Again.")

There are many reasons why mission statements are necessary, but there isn't one good reason why companies shouldn't be held to the standards they set up in their mission statements. With its Mission Review process, Starbucks continues to practice what it preaches, living its mission because its employees wouldn't settle for anything less.

Leading Questions . . .

- Can you recite your company's mission statement without looking it up? Better yet, can you understand enough to act on it? Even better still, when was the last time you even thought to review your company's mission statement?
- Are your employees engaged in the company's mission? How do you know?
- How does your company adhere to the mission and goals it sets for itself?
- Does your company have a mission review process where company criticism and recommendations are accepted? What could you do to encourage a more open atmosphere where employees could be heard and acknowledged within your business?

Practice Passionate Followership

Not everyone can be a leader all the time. Yet in business we've been trained to lead or get out of the way. Not at Starbucks. Some of the best, most effective Starbucks employees are passionate followers more than they are leaders.

One of the first lessons learned when new employees join Starbucks is that the company values passionate followers more than it does passionate leaders. By no means does Starbucks dismiss the importance of leadership. Leadership is important to the company's success. But followership is just as vital.

Followership doesn't mean blindly following others. Nor does it mean forgoing thinking for acting. What it does mean is that when decisions are made, Starbucks' employees should respect the decision and work toward achieving what has been decided. In other words, more energy should be spent working for decisions and not against them.

One of the core values at Starbucks, and at many mission-driven companies today, is the concept of *servant leadership*. The term was popularized by Robert Greenleaf, which he wrote about in many of his books, including *Servant Leadership* and *Servant As Leader*. Greenleaf's concept was inspired, in part, by a story by Herman Hesse in his book, *Journey to the East*. In it, Hesse tells about a league of travelers taking a mystical journey in search of enlightenment. With them is a servant, Leo, who takes care of their needs and performs their menial tasks, but who also sustains and guides them with his wisdom, insight, and presence. When Leo unexpectedly leaves them, they are unable to continue on and disband amid discord. Many years later, the narrator, one of the original group, retraces his steps in an attempt to chronicle their journey. He happens upon Leo, whom he discovers is the spiritual head, a great and respected leader, of the order that sponsored his group's journey.

Greenleaf's point in drawing on this story is to illustrate the importance of being a servant to those whom you would lead. His belief was that legitimate leadership can exist only when those who are being led choose to follow, rather than being compelled or coerced to; that leaders seek to be servants first and leadership flows naturally from their role as servant.

Servant leadership provides a couple of critical insights for organizations who want a committed, engaged workforce: (1) Passionate followership is founded upon a willingness and enthusiasm on the part of those being led—if you want passionate employees, you've got to serve them first; and (2) leadership can come in many forms, and anyone who serves the needs and wants of others has the potential to be a leader also—in other words, *leaders* and *followers* are not mutually exclusive.

For years, Starbucks has held day-long seminars in which store managers are trained to become more servant-leader–minded. Specifically, the trainers focus on three qualities: empathy, listening, and authenticity. Empathy is a critical character trait that Starbucks expects its partners to embody. You can't serve people's needs and wants if you're not empathetic to their wishes and desires. A key part of this concept is the ability to listen. Listening to what your employees, supervisors, and customers are really saying is crucial to understanding what they want. And the ability to be authentic and true to your character in all situations, no matter the stress level, is the final quality. Empathy, listening, and authenticity are three major servant-leadership skills taught to all store-level managers.

Starbucks expects a lot from its employees, and it gives a lot in return. By making clear what it takes to succeed within the company, Starbucks lays the foundation for employees to opt in to the company's mission, becoming passionate followers and leaders along the way.

Leading Questions . . .

- List employees in your department or company that lead by serving others. What might you do to better emulate the leadership style of those co-workers you've just listed?
- Would your employees work at your company if they didn't need to?

People Quit People (Not Companies)

At Starbucks, it's believed bad bosses hurt the company far more than bad business decisions. When Starbucks employees leave the company, they do so far more often because of a bad manager than they do because of bad business management.

The relationship between a Starbucks employee and his or her manager is the most critical factor impacting that employee's work performance, on-the-job happiness, and longevity with the company. That's because, for all of the high-sounding rhetoric, passion, and commitment of the company's leadership, to a front-line employee, his or her boss *is* the company. The barista's store manager represents Starbucks more than Howard Schultz or anyone else. By the same token, the baristas represent Starbucks to the stores' customers more than any other people, and more than any marketing promotion or message.

The best bosses at Starbucks find ways to manage their people and not their projects. Starbucks employees are more willing to overachieve and deliver outstanding results when their managers give them space to work on the business without meddling in *their* business.

These bosses are also experts at championing the ideas of the employees who report directly to them, that is, their "direct reports." They can shepherd ideas through the corporate hairball decision-making process to pave the way for making ideas from their team happen.

The most respected and admired managers at Starbucks take seriously their responsibility for giving performance evaluations. They view job appraisals as a time to develop the skills of their direct reports, prepping them for a promotion. These managers understand when their direct reports look good, the managers look even better. It's a matter of pride for these bosses to see members of their team promoted within the company, no matter if it means that an employee might leave, creating a major hole to fill within their department.

Finally, the best bosses at Starbucks are expert "firefighters." When all hell breaks loose with a project, and invariably hell will break loose, the best bosses at Starbucks are the first to put on their firefighting hats and get their hands dirty to solve the problem.

In 2001, Seattle was rocked by an earthquake that registered a 6.9 on the Richter scale. Starbucks' headquarters building was extensively damaged and was cut off from its stores for a short time. Even after contact was re-established, it would take a while for things to get back to normal. The Starbucks operations team, a department serving the vital role of communicating with stores on a daily basis, had to take refuge in a training room at the old roasting plant in Seattle. There were 45 people cramped inside one room for six months, connected to the outside world by T1 lines and cell phones. The partners on the operations team did a remarkable job under tough circumstances, oftentimes meeting in people's homes, figuring out how to keep thousands of stores functioning smoothly despite the circumstances and generally working together as a team.

But one of the most important outcomes of this challenging situation in Seattle was what we learned about the managers at the store level. We learned that the partners in the field could be trusted to make things happen and make excellent decisions without much hand-holding or direct control from above. Despite the entrepreneurial culture at Starbucks, it has always been a heavy, top-down, centralized organization. What this calamity taught us was that there was a great deal more resourcefulness and know-how than we had given our field managers credit for.

People quit people, not companies. It's the person on the ground, not the board of directors on the eighth floor of corporate headquarters, who represents the company to your employees. By the same logic, people will stay loyal to people who are resourceful, passionate, caring, and respectful.

Leading Questions . . .

- How does your company's turnover rate compare to that of your industry's rate?
- Are performance evaluations given on time? Are they productive and conducted in an open, clearly defined manner?
- Would your lower-level managers and employees function well if you weren't there? How do you know?

Brands Are Made Possible by People

Ambitious coffee competitors like Caribou Coffee, Cosi's, Tully's Coffee, Gloria Jean's, CC's Coffee House, and others have all tried to mimic Starbucks' success in some way. And they have all fallen short in some way.

These coffee companies have tried and are trying to replicate the products and experiences Starbucks delivers, but they can't replicate the people Starbucks has delivering the products and experiences to customers.

Products do not create brands, people create brands. It's the people that matter more in creating a brand than the product itself. And Starbucks places a tremendous emphasis on hiring the right people to deliver exceptional products and meaningful experiences to customers.

When hiring employees for store-level and corporate-level positions, Starbucks looks for the following upstanding "people" qualities in each candidate: genuineness, conscientiousness, knowledge, and involvement.

GENUINENESS

Genuine people build solid relationships with others because they are approachable and likeable. Starbucks employees who are genuine make for great team members, and they can be trusted to deliver heartfelt customer service.

CONSCIENTIOUSNESS

Conscientious employees are considerate and pay attention to seemingly insignificant details because everything matters to them. And because "everything matters" at Starbucks, this quality is of utmost importance in all employees Starbucks chooses to hire.

KNOWLEDGE

Starbucks employees are expected to know coffee to the extent that they will confidently share their coffee knowledge with customers. To find employees with this quality, Starbucks looks for people who ask questions. Asking questions at Starbucks is not a sign of weakness. It's a sign of strength. Inquisitive employees lead to knowledgeable employees, and knowledgeable employees are quicker to share their expertise with others.

INVOLVEMENT

Employees who get involved within the company and within their community are valued at Starbucks. When employees take the time to get involved and make connections with others, they showcase a caring soul. Starbucks seeks to hire caring souls because they are more likely to make emotional connections with people.

Starbucks was founded by people passionate about elevating coffee from a dull routine to an invigorating and relaxing escape; and it attracted others—employees, as well as customers—who wanted to participate in accomplishing this mission.

One of Starbucks' regional competitors, Tully's, was started in 1992 by a real-estate developer who had helped Starbucks expand into some of the best locations in the Pacific Northwest. Tully's had witnessed first-hand the rise of Starbucks and so reasoned it could replicate their "blueprint" for success. And Tully's has succeeded, to an extent. Tully's has good coffee and a pleasant atmosphere and tries to focus on providing a coffee experience similar to the Starbucks experience. The fundamental difference, however, is that Tully's was founded with the mission (though not stated) of capitalizing on the boom in gourmet coffeehouses that Starbucks inspired, in Seattle and around the country. Ultimately, their "me too" positioning rings hollow. They've exploited an opportunity to make money, but are they following their passion? Will their employees have the same "passion"?

The people behind the Starbucks brand know that customers want to be able to relate to your product, your service, and your company on a human level—it's a concept that ties back to the idea in Tribal Truth #4, "Tell the Story. Don't Make Up a Story." This concept of relating to customers on a human level is not just limited to businesses with a direct service component. The next time you're at the grocery store, examine the packaging of the different products. Pick up a bag of flour—what could possibly be more commoditized than something as simple as flour? Well, if you happen to check out a bag of King Arthur Flour, you may be surprised to find that even flour can be made personal. A 100-percent employee-owned, 200-year-old company with a fanatical commitment to quality (sound familiar?), King Arthur communicates its story on every package and convinces you that, indeed, all flours are not the same. Suddenly, a commoditized product has become personal—you feel the care and passion of the people who milled the flour and who have gone out of their way to bring it to you.

There are many examples of companies whose products embody and communicate the passion of their people— Ben & Jerry's, The Body Shop, Apple Computer, Southwest Airlines—and you recognize it when you see it.

Passion can't be manufactured and it will not survive if it is artificial. It must be organic. And one advantage Starbucks will always have over its competitors—the advantage any company can have if it hires and inspires the right people—is the passion of their employees.

Brands are made possible by people because, unlike products and services, competitors cannot replicate a brand's people, or their passion.

Leading Questions . . .

- How does your company capitalize on the passion of its employees?
- Do your customers get a sense of the people behind the products and services from your marketing communications, packaging, and so on?

Abhor Complacency.
Resist Conservatism.
Fight Conceit.

But the path for innovation needs to be consistent with who
we are—the protagonist for coffee's past, present, and future.
We are not about culture. We are about great coffee experiences.
It so happens that for hundreds of years these experiences
have involved reading, music, culinary experiences,
community, self-discovery, and creative inspiration.
That is our link to culture. We have only begun to mine it.

SCOTT BEDBURY,
former Starbucks executive
(internal Starbucks presentation)

With supreme market dominance, and not a real
competitive threat in sight, one would think Starbucks
could ease up a little on its frantic pace. Starbucks has essentially cornered the market on all things coffee, and
momentum alone should allow them to reach their stated
goal of at least 30,000 locations worldwide.

But the cultural mindset of Starbucks is one that believes that at any time this could all come crashing down.

Starbucks insiders maintain a feeling the marketplace may suddenly turn from loving lattes to exiling espresso.

In many ways, Starbucks still behaves like the upstart coffee company it was. They've managed to keep the start-up mentality alive by not succumbing to the Three Cs of Complacency, Conservatism, and Conceit. These Three Cs have derailed many a successful, growing business.

COMPLACENCY

Complacency is self-satisfied contentment with the status quo. It's doing nothing new so as not to disrupt the supposedly good thing going on. A complacent Starbucks would never have launched Frappuccino® blended beverages in 1995. Instead, it would have been satisfied with merely offering iced versions of its hot lattes. Without Frappuccino blended beverages on its menu, Starbucks would be a much smaller business today as the Frappuccino category comprises up to 20 percent of a store's total yearly sales.

A complacent Starbucks would not be continuing its decade-long attempts to grow a lunch business. And while Starbucks still sees coffee as the core of its business, it sees food as the opportunity. In an effort to increase daytime traffic between 10:00 AM and 2:00 PM, the company has put a lot of time and money into providing sandwiches and other lunchtime faire. Starbucks hasn't cracked this code just yet, but it's willing to keep trying.

Trying new things, thinking in different ways, will keep corporate complacency away from a business. Yes, some new things will fail, and some will work with great success. The yin and yang of a dynamic business is what keeps it interesting, keeps it compelling, and keeps it successful.

CONSERVATISM

Businesses that stop taking risks have become conservative in their decision-making. When a company becomes conservative, it makes decisions based on *maintaining* what they have and not *growing* what they have.

A conservative Starbucks would never have become involved in the music business through its Hear Music® business. Sure, customers liked the music playing in-store, but expecting them to buy CDs at a coffee shop was a risk, a risk that is paying off handsomely as Starbucks is gaining sales and credibility as a music retailer.

The company continued its risk-taking mentality by pairing Starbucks Entertainment, the same division responsible for the Hear Music label, with film producer and distributor Lions Gate to market *Akeelah and the Bee*. This was a new avenue for Starbucks Entertainment, one that a conservative company would not ever venture into. The pairing gave Lions Gate unique access to Starbucks customers, a knowledgeable base who fits *Akeelah's* projected demographics well. For Starbucks, it was an opportunity to introduce an independent film it believed in to its customers without the usual fast-food movie tie-ins, such as action figures and hit-you-over-the-head gimmicks. As Howard Schultz told forbes.com just before the movie opened in April 2006, "Just as we have demonstrated with music, we believe that Starbucks can ultimately change the rules of the game for film marketing and distribution."[1] Starbucks baristas prescreened the movie, giving the partnership hope that the power of Starbucks' word-of-mouth campaigns will pay off.

There is no guarantee that either of these Starbucks Entertainment moves will succeed in the long run, but failure is also far from certain. That's the beauty of risk-taking. Companies free from conservatism can explore—and succeed—in ventures that others would never, ever touch.

CONCEIT

Conceit causes businesses to make decisions based more upon internal business needs and less upon external end-user customer needs.

A conceited Starbucks would never have responded to demands of activist groups by offering hormone-free milk and Fair Trade Certified™ coffee. Though customer demand for hormone-free milk and fair trade coffee is small, it is growing.

The fair trade discussion is one that is still high on the minds of Starbucks' executives and Starbucks' opponents. While Starbucks wants to please its customers, and it wants to pay farmers what they deserve, it will not compromise quality and taste. Starbucks buys the best arabica beans available to maintain its high standards in taste. That is its first priority—giving customers the taste and high quality customers expect. Starbucks will not compromise its coffee quality standards just so the company can buy more fair trade coffees. Currently, the Fair Trade Certified coffees offered at Starbucks represent a small fraction of total coffee sales and much of what Starbucks purchases is not sold as Fair Trade Certified coffee but is used in its coffee blends like Starbucks House Blend. However, as fair trade coffee beans improve in quality, so will the quantity of Fair Trade Certified beans sold in Starbucks.

Starbucks understands the importance of doing the right things right, and the right thing means giving customers the choice of more socially responsible milk and farmer-friendly coffee offerings. It listens to criticism and suggestions and responds, knowing that customers can always tell when a company is operating in its own interest or in the interest of its customers.

Being able to resist the Three Cs has kept Starbucks dynamic and involved in its own industry and in the global marketplace. Above all, it has shown when employees take risks, think big, and stay humble (no matter how great the level of success) any business can stay on track and in touch.

Leading Questions . . .

- List some risky endeavors your business has attempted in the past 12 months. Why did some succeed while others failed?
- How has conservatism manifested itself within your business?
- Has being conceited prevented your company from doing a worthwhile venture? What must be done to change the attitude of conceit at your business?
- What new programs must your company begin to better fight corporate complacency?
- Is there something your customers have been asking your company to provide? How is your company responding?

Build Bridges Between Old Employees and New Employees

Brands can get bigger without destroying what they once were.
They just need to connect the past to the future.

SCOTT BEDBURY,
former Starbucks executive
(A New Brand World)

As businesses grow, so does the need to hire more people to handle the increasing workload. Eventually all growing companies face the situation of needing to combine the talents and perspectives of long-time (old-school) employees with those of recently hired (new-school) employees. Integrating this influx of new hires with long-timers has been one of the greatest challenges Starbucks has faced in growing its business.

A company will not realize its future if it doesn't understand its past. Old-school employees are able to maintain the company's connection to its roots as well as serve the

valuable role of helping indoctrinate new school employees to the cause.

At the same time, it's very easy, as an old school employee, to discredit the ideas of someone who hasn't ma-
tured in the company. This is especially true for a
company like Starbucks, where people who started in the
late 1980s or early 1990s helped the company grow up
and grow global. Even today, with the fast pace of Starbucks' growth, it's easy to feel that a mere few years ren-
dered the experience of decades. That's great to foster a
sense of ownership, but it's also an easy way for folks to get
set in their ways.

Through trial and error, Starbucks has learned how to
bridge old-school thought with new-school thinking. The
following bridge-building lessons learned are simple but
important for growing companies to follow.

OFFER SOLUTIONS, NOT OBSTACLES

When batting around ideas in meetings, old-school
employees need to be careful not to say, "Yeah, but that'll
never work. We tried it a few years ago." Instead, old-
school employees need to learn to say "Yes . . . and." As
in, "Yes, and we will need to solve for this issue because
last time we did something similar and things didn't work
as expected." This does two things, it lets the new employees know what the current concerns are, and it gives

a glimpse of company history—in this case, why the idea might be met with some resistance by someone else.

BE A TEACHER

While new employees have the chance to share the experiences they gain at other companies, old-school employees need to take the time to teach new-school employees nuances about the culture of the business. For example, every Starbucks meeting used to begin with a coffee tasting. During these tastings, partners would celebrate and discuss coffee much like wine enthusiasts discuss wine. Admittedly, it's impractical to start every meeting with a coffee tasting, but old-school partners would find ways to make it happen. And now, many new-school partners are keeping the company tradition alive by ensuring coffee tastings happen before meetings.

LISTEN FIRST, REACT SECOND

We've all seen this scenario before where a new hire comes in with guns blazing away and shoots himself or herself in the mouth by saying too much too soon. New-school employees should spend more time listening and less time reacting during their initial stages of employment. An unwritten rule at Starbucks was to wait at least six weeks before speaking up with strong opinions during meetings. A whole lot can happen in six weeks, mostly the opportunity to learn about the corporate culture and enough about the company's past to anticipate likely reactions to new ideas.

Of course, new-school employees are hired for a reason—they have valuable experience gleaned from other fields and businesses. Their ideas and their approach to thinking often is what got them hired in the first place. Following the six-week rule goes the extra step into solidifying the credibility of any new hire because it shows that the new school employee values the existing culture and wants to learn about it before offering powerful changes.

BEFRIEND AN OLD-SCHOOL EMPLOYEE

Starbucks establishes mentor/mentee relationships for many executives coming from the outside. So many times, when new managers come into a company, they believe the best tactic to gain respect is by spouting tough opinions and issuing strong solutions. They feel they have to prove themselves to justify their new positions. Starbucks avoids this by assigning new managers to mentors, other executives with 8 to 10 years of experience, often having worked their way up the Starbucks ranks. Being teamed with those who are used to working in a people-focused culture markedly helps the transition from outsider to company-, community-, and employee-focused partner.

Through these relationships, outside executives are able to better learn the cultural dos and don'ts of the company. As a result, fewer entry level partners flameout, and instead they go on to make significant contributions to the company for years on end. Befriending a long-time employee is an easy step that the savviest new-school Starbucks people make happen.

Leading Questions . . .

- What does your company do to integrate new employees into the company culture?
- How well was the most recent new thought employee welcomed into the company? Would you like this person's experience duplicated with the next new hire?

Hire Passion over Experience

"It is better to hire people who can get you to where you want to be than people who profess to have been there before." That's brilliant advice from Guy Kawasaki, old-school Apple Computer employee, as written in his book, *The Macintosh Way*. It also highlights the Starbucks' way of hiring right.

Starbucks places more importance on hiring people who have a mix of verve, candor, can-do spirit, and a highly likeable personality than they do on people who have years of experience.

Back in 2001, Starbucks brought in a new chief marketing officer (CMO) with loads of experience—Quaker Oats, General Foods, Sunbeam, and so on—but very little understanding of Starbucks' unique culture or trust in those she was brought in to lead. She immediately began to ruffle the feathers of the people who had been successfully building one of the most successful brands in the world. Instead of trying harder to catch their passion, she dismissed the people working under her as inexperienced and naïve. Refusing to listen to others that she felt knew less than she did, the CMO barked orders, exerted more control, and brought in highly paid, outside consultants to do the creative marketing work that was "beyond" the capabilities of her own internal team.

Of course, the outside consultants weren't passionate about coffee or the Starbucks experience. The new CMO was doing things the way she was used to doing them. She wasn't going to tolerate new ideas that might not work, as mistakes were not something she was going to stand for. Of course, the mistakes were often what taught us more about the brand than the successes. But sometimes people with an abundance of experience have a dearth of humility, and they honestly feel that they have nothing left to learn.

The CMO lasted about five months before being let go, and gone were the new creative consultants. All the less-experienced, passionate marketers remained and went about making things happen.

Starbucks has learned experienced people find ways to say "No, it can't be done" more easily because they've invariably tried (and failed at) something similar in a different life. While passionate people, operating under refreshing naïveté, will find ways to say "Yes" and not be inhibited by the ripples of past failures. At Starbucks, it's simple: The right people to hire have more passion than they do experience.

Leading Questions . . .

- What qualities do you look for and screen for in the hiring process? Do you immediately eliminate potentially talented candidates solely based on their lack of experience?

TRIBAL TRUTH 41

Participation Is the Price of Admission

Thou shalt not stand idly by.

HOWARD BEHAR,
former Starbucks executive
(internal Starbucks presentation)

How many times have you sat idle in meetings or in conferences? Instead of participating, you choose to disengage yourself and simply coast.

Coasting will not get you far at Starbucks. Your career will stagnate. You will get left behind. You will eventually get ejected.

The most successful Starbucks partners realize participation is the price of admission to meetings and conferences.

When Starbucks partners choose to accept an invitation to a meeting, they choose to come prepared to make a worthwhile contribution. They choose to offer their insights. They choose to ask the tough questions. They choose to participate.

By participating, these partners not only become a part of the consensus-building environment. They also help themselves get recognized as someone who cares about the business and as someone who is eager to make things happen.

The cost of participation is that, sometimes, you will bring up unpleasant truths, pose challenging questions, or zig when the rest of your team is zagging. In the moment, this can make you feel uncomfortable, like you aren't a part of the team. No one wants to be seen as someone who only shoots down ideas, poking holes in every new strategy or initiative. But in my experience, as someone who was always willing to stick his neck out or go against the grain if it meant avoiding making a bad decision, it was always worth it in the long run, even if, in the short term, I was worried about being seen as less of a team player.

But many have a hard time seeing the wisdom of this strategy. And, as a result, they hang back, declining to put in their two cents or sound the warning, afraid of what the others will think. Ironically, this fear of being ostracized can often lead groups into making decisions they all know are wrong. In his classic book, *The Abilene Paradox*, Jerry Harvey described a group dynamic in which every member of the team privately agrees what to do, and yet—because each fears being rejected by the others—they all openly agree to do the opposite. His contention was that managing conflict in organizations was far less critical than managing *agreement*.

Fostering an environment in which dissent is welcomed, not scorned, empowers employees, makes them active participants in the decision-making process, and creates eager, enthusiastic, more successful partners.

Participation is the price of admission to any meeting or any business gathering. Don't procrastinate. Participate.

Leading Questions . . .

- How is participation by employees encouraged in your company?
- How is it discouraged?

Encourage
Healthy Dialogue

What happens when you gather a roomful of passion-ate, and sometimes highly caffeinated, overachieving Starbucks partners in a meeting? You get *healthy dialogue*.

Starbucks has a peaceful business veneer, but behind closed doors in any of its more than 100 conference rooms at its Seattle headquarters, you will witness heated and contested conversations.

Starbucks would rather have these difficult conversa-tions take place in conference rooms than in hallways. That's because Starbucks' consensus-building, decision-making culture requires that all issues from all angles be discussed before a decision is reached. This cannot hap-pen in a hallway conversation between only a few people.

In response to a rash of unhealthy hallway conversa-tions that were undermining the effectiveness of Star-bucks project teams in the early 2000s, then-CEO Orin Smith posted "Effective Meeting Rules" signs in every conference room. These rules were designed to refocus and encourage healthy discussion for all Starbucks project team meetings.

For Starbucks, an effective meeting adheres to the following seven rules. It must:

1. Have clear objectives
2. Follow a focused agenda
3. Begin and end on time
4. Have a designated leader and attendees who have clear roles
5. Foster open, honest discussion
6. Communicate next steps and responsibilities
7. Fulfill its objectives

Leading Questions . . .

- Are meetings something that employees in your company look forward to or dread?
- How productive are meetings in your company? Is there healthy dialogue within them? Do decisions get made there or elsewhere?

Radically Simplify Your Organizational Chart

When companies grow, their organizational charts also grow. Business growth spawns newly created and highly reorganized departments that transform a once-simple organizational chart into a labyrinth of boxes connected via a series of straight and dashed lines. Starbucks is no exception.

Whenever Starbucks undergoes a major corporate reorganization and redraws its organizational structure, which usually happens once every 18 months, executive management does two things. First, Starbucks executives remind corporate employees that while their proverbial cheese has been moved, employees must not hem and haw about the changes. Instead, Starbucks employees should scurry about and sniff around to adjust to the new organizational alignment.

The second thing Starbucks executives do is remind employees that no matter what organizational and departmental management changes take place, there is only one boss that truly matters—the customer. If you wanted to illustrate what this would look like in terms of your organizational chart, you would see a straight line going from the customer to each and every employee, no matter his or her place in the corporate hierarchy:

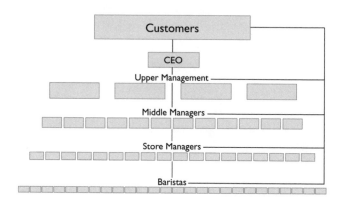

To make it simple, Starbucks hammers home the point by dusting off and distributing the following radically streamlined, vintage organizational chart from deep inside the company's cultural chambers:

It's natural that with growth comes more complexity in organizational structures—specifically, that there are more people in the middle, overseeing these employees and reporting to those supervisors. What Starbucks realizes is that nowhere, in most organizational charts, is a box for the customer. At Starbucks, no matter where you are in the organizational chart, there is a direct line connecting you to the customer, a line that bypasses all other lines of the company hierarchy.

The Starbucks culture believes there is only one organizational chart that truly matters to a customer-first business, and that one has every employee symbolically reporting to the real boss—the customer.

Leading Questions . . .

- Is your company's organizational chart simple and easy for everyone to understand? Does it make sense to people who work in the company?
- Where is the customer in your company's organizational chart?

TRIBAL TRUTH 44

Always Measure Your Comparable Job Performance

Many overachieving Starbucks partners measure their *comparable job performance*. They do it in the same way businesses and financial analysts look at year-over-year comparable sales growth (comp sales) to gauge the vitality of a business and evaluate its future growth prospects.

By comparing their current job performance in relation to their job performance of the previous year, these overachieving Starbucks partners are able to better evaluate their contribution in the workplace to determine if their overall performance is trending positively or negatively.

What if you were to figuratively measure your comparable job performance? Would you find yourself performing 2 percent better this year compared to last year? Or have you performed 20 percent better? Perhaps your comparable job performance is trending negatively.

Before your next job appraisal, take some time to figuratively measure your comparable job performance.

Note that some measures are objective and quantifiable while others are purely subjective and rely on your own judgment. That's okay. Measuring your comparable job performance is simply another self-evaluation tool—one that focuses on your annual progress, as opposed to against a static standard. Honest and candid self-reflection are critical here, not whether or not you think you improved by 10 percent or 20 percent.

To start measuring your comparable job performance, ask yourself the following questions:

- How much more did you contribute to the success of your company this year compared to last?
- Have you gained more responsibility in the past year?
- Are you more confident in your abilities to positively impact your company's future?
- Did you lead or participate in more project teams this year than last?
- Were you involved in more worthwhile projects this year?
- Did you deliver more of your projects on time, on budget, and on strategy this year?
- Do you have more direct reports this year than last?
- What steps did you take in the past year to learn new skills?

- Do your peers have greater respect for your contribution as an employee and as a person this year compared to last year?
- Have you made more of a difference in the lives of your direct reports or peers this year than last?
- Do you feel more satisfied personally and professionally this year?

After reviewing your comparable job performance from the previous year, you then need to develop action steps in order to set the stage for positively comparing against yourself in next year.

If you expect to perform 20 percent better this upcoming year than last year, you will need to figure out how you are going to achieve your comparable performance growth goal. You may determine you should attend a seminar to learn new skills. Perhaps reading a business book will give you insight so that you can perform better on the job. Alternatively, you may need to gain an assignment on a different project to increase your responsibility and visibility. Or it may be a case of simply working smarter and not harder.

The value in measuring your comparable job performance cannot be understated—it will allow you to better determine on-the-job activities so you can learn more, grow faster, and prosper truer in both your professional-life and your personal-life.

Leading Questions . . .

- What kind of performance review system does your company have in place?
- If there is a self-review component to your performance review, does it examine comparable job performance from one year to the next? If not, how could you incorporate a review that measures employees' progress?

Marketing Has Two Audiences

*It's not one thing, but a lot of things. It's not good enough
to have a good ad, but everything you do helps complete
the circle . . . the packaging, the community involvement,
the service all help build that emotional connection."*

HOWARD SCHULTZ
*("The Art of Creating Passionate Consumers,"
KNOW, spring/summer 2005, p. 14.)*

Do you think all the posters, banners, brochures, and
other marketing signage you see in Starbucks are meant solely
for customers? Think again, as marketing at Starbucks impacts more than just customers . . . it also impacts employees.

Sure, Starbucks uses its in-store signage to promote
seasonal beverages, whole bean coffees, and pastries with
hopes of triggering impulse purchases from customers.
However, customer focus groups have told Starbucks they
do not necessarily rely upon the marketing signage to influence their purchase decisions. Instead, customers rely upon

the opinions of baristas behind the counter to influence which beverages, beans, and pastries they buy.

With that understanding, Starbucks uses its in-store signage to influence the opinions of Starbucks' baristas.

For example, the many brochures Starbucks displays at the condiment bar are noticed more by employees than by customers. Customers rarely read these brochures, which range from descriptions of whole bean coffees to marketing promotions with T-Mobile and Visa to Starbucks' environmental efforts. But all employees at some point read these brochures—whether out of company adoration or break-time boredom.

Even the banner sign that is strategically positioned in the pathway of customers walking to the counter has a greater impact on employees than customers. Starbucks employees see that banner sign every day of every week they work and automatically know the product focus of the current marketing campaign.

Marketing signage can be used to inform and inspire employees, who can then better influence purchase decisions made by customers.

Leading Questions . . .

- When you craft your company's and products' marketing messages, do you take into account how they will be received by employees?
- Do you seek feedback from employees on how effective the marketing and promotional materials are?

Some
Parting Truths

Profit is a By-Product

Starbucks doesn't view profit and the maximizing of profits as business strategy. The company views profit as an outcome. The mindset at Starbucks is, profit happens as a direct result of doing everything else right . . .

Profit happens when a business focuses on building its business to create its brand.

Profit happens when a business strives to be the best and not the biggest.

Profit happens when the actions of a business speak louder than its advertising.

Profit happens when a business is designed to satisfy customers' aspirations and not to merely meet customers' basic needs.

Profit happens when it fosters devotion more than loyalty from customers.

Profit happens when a business connects, discovers, and responds to its customers.

Profit happens when a business makes its company easy to believe in.

Profit happens when a business develops a company culture which abhors complacency, resists conservatism, and fights conceit.

Profit happens when a business does everything else right.

Be Mission-Driven to Change the World

[Starbucks' goal is] to become an enduring, great company with the most recognized and respected brand in the world, known for inspiring and nurturing the human spirit.

THE STARBUCKS BHAG (BIG HAIRY AUDACIOUS GOAL)
(internal Starbucks presentation, Seattle)

There is only one worthwhile reason to start a new business or launch a new product, and that is to change the world.

Sure, changing the world is a daunting task for any entrepreneur or brand manager to add to their to-do list.

But that's what Starbucks did.

Starbucks changed how the world drinks and appreciates coffee. Admittedly, the original founders of Starbucks had no idea their passion for changing how Seattle-ites drink and appreciate dark-roasted coffee would ultimately change the world. But it has.

From its inception and to this day and into tomorrow, Starbucks is mission-driven to make a difference in the world.

Each year, 700,000 new businesses are started[1] and 30,000 new products are launched in the United States. Do we really need that many new businesses and new products? Obviously not, because 70 percent of all new businesses fail within 24 months and 75 percent of new products fail within 2 years of being launched.[2]

Given those grim statistics, why even bother launching a new business or new service if it is not going to change the world. Seriously, why even bother?

What purpose is behind your next business? What purpose is behind your next service?

Starbucks Tribal Knowledge tells us the only worthwhile way to thrive in today's hyper-competitive business environment is to set out to change the world with your new business, new product, and/or new service. After all . . . that's what Starbucks did.

From Ideas
to Implementation

After every Tribal Truth, you were asked a few leading questions, and hopefully you've gained new perspectives about your business from asking and thinking about those questions. Now, to help you shape those new perspectives and turn them into ideas ready for action, consider working through the following Action Steps:

UNO: A FEW ACTIONS STEPS
ABOUT THE BUSINESS OF BRANDING
AND THE BRANDING OF BUSINESS

As we learned, Starbucks became the company it is today not by building its brand but rather by building its business to create the brand. Instead of spending marketing dollars on making better commercials, Starbucks marketers spent those dollars on making better customer experiences. Generally speaking, this is how Starbucks goes about building its brand.

For your business to go about building its brand in much the same way, follow these Action Steps:

1. Declare how your business will change the world. (It doesn't have to be the whole world, just a small corner of the world you do business in.)
2. Examine your current marketing programs and determine what needs to be improved, altered, or deleted altogether in order to follow through on your declaration.
3. Define all the project Actions Steps that need to be done by when and by whom.
4. Enlist the assistance of influential people within your company who will help you better champion these marketing programs in order to receive the go-ahead from the ultimate decision-makers within your company.

DUE: A FEW ACTION STEPS ABOUT DELIVERING MEMORABLE CUSTOMER EXPERIENCES

The experience matters at Starbucks. To create memorable customer experiences, Starbucks strives to over-deliver on all its promises made to customers. Starbucks also treats its customers not as tourists seeking superficial trinkets but as explorers seeking meaningful stories. Starbucks knows remarkable things get remarked about, so it does remarkable things in hopes that customers will tell their friends and family about their memorable customer experience at Starbucks.

To start delivering memorable customer experiences within your company, use these Action Steps:

1. Stop thinking like a marketer and start thinking like a customer. Do this by assigning different people within your company the task of spending a day being a "regular" customer. Have them all buy products from your company and from at least two other direct competitors, as well as two unrelated businesses. Require them to write up a short report outlining their shopping experiences as they related to how each of their five senses (sight, hearing, touch, smell, and taste) were (or were not) engaged during each shopping visit. In addition, have them note the two main takeaways they experienced from each place they shopped.

2. Conduct a postmortem following the shopping experience assignment and discuss the takeaways from each person's shopping experience. Based off the discussion, compile three lists of activities your company should STOP DOING, START DOING, and CONTINUE DOING.

3. Refine your STOP/START/CONTINUE list by evaluating the feasibility and remarkability of each

activity on the list. Discard the unfeasible and unremarkable activities.

4. Activate your refined STOP/START/CONTINUE list by following steps 3 and 4 listed in the previous *Uno* Action Steps and you will be on a much better path of delivering memorable customer experiences.

TRE: A FEW ACTION STEPS ABOUT CREATING THE KIND OF WORKPLACE YOU'D LIKE TO WORK IN

Starbucks understands a business cannot exceed the expectations of its customers without first exceeding the expectations of its employees. In many ways, Starbucks spends more time and money marketing to its employees than to its customers. Passion is a driving force within the company culture of Starbucks as it is the passions of employees that truly fuel Starbucks' success.

Creating a workplace you'd like to work in is an ongoing challenge. Here are a few Action Steps to get you started creating such a place:

1. Listen to your employees. Start designing ways in which your employees can submit ideas on how to improve the employee experience.

2. Respond to all employee-submitted ideas. It is unrealistic to implement all the ideas employees send in, but it is realistic (and very important) to respond to every employee who submits an idea.

3. Determine how much money your company spent last year on customer-focused initiatives (ranging from product development to marketing programs) and compare it to how much the company spent on employee-focused initiatives (ranging from training programs to incentive contests to costs associated with employee benefits). If the discrepancy is wide in favor of customers, consider ways to bring about a better balance between customer-focused spending and employee-focused spending.

Join the Conversation: Learn through Sharing

FROM TEN TO TENS OF MILLIONS . . .

Throughout my marketing career I've been quick to share interesting articles and ideas with others. On Monday mornings back in the day, I would usually find myself wrestling with the office copy machine to churn out double-sided copies of must-read articles from *Fast Company*, *BusinessWeek*, *The Wall Street Journal*, and copies of ideas from a variety of other sources. At that time, my distribution list consisted of only ten coworkers.

These days I'm still sharing interesting articles and ideas with others, but the difference is my distribution list extends beyond ten coworkers to tens of millions of people on the Internet (and now to thousands reading this book).

Thanks to the expansive reach of blogs and to blogging's ease-of-use, I no longer spend my Monday mornings slaving over a problematic copy machine to share articles and ideas. Instead, blogging allows me to simply share stuff online and digitally "cc:" the entire online world and not just my marketing coworkers.

SEE YA, CC: . . .

cc: is shorthand for "carbon copy." Long before the emergence of word processors and photocopiers, typewriters ruled the written world, and making carbon copies was the everyday way to share important documents with others.

To make a duplicate copy during the typewriter age, one had to slip a piece of carbon paper in between two pieces of paper, and after finishing typing, one was left with an original copy and a *carbon copy.*

The original meaning of the term *cc:* is irrelevant now, but its intent is highly relevant today. We use cc: everyday when we send messages to multiple recipients through email. We even use cc: as a verb, as in, "I cc:'d so and so."

But the term *cc:* is so yesterday, while the term *dc:* is so today.

We've evolved from making carbon copies to creating *digital copies.* And through blogging, we can digitally cc: the whole wide world.

SHARING TO LEARN . . .

The main reason I blog is to learn—that's because I learn by sharing. Conversation always follows sharing, and inherent in any conversation is the art of listening and the act of responding.

When you passionately share your opinions, thoughts, and influences with others on a blog posting, it will usually generate comments.

I learn when someone openly challenges my thoughts, as it forces me to reevaluate my thinking. I also learn when someone adds their unique perspective by riffing off my perspective. It's through the exchange of listening and responding that I learn best.

But before you can share to learn, you must learn to share.

LEARNING TO SHARE . . .

Too many times we find it easier to keep our opinions, thoughts, and influences to ourselves. Blogging requires you to tear down barriers and be more transparent in sharing with others what you are passionate about.

The act of blogging has been characterized by some as egotistical selfish musings. I could not disagree more.

Blogging is as selfless an act as one can do. To blog is to be transparent. To blog is to open oneself up to being judged. To blog is to share. And to share is to learn.

THE VIRTUOUS CYCLE OF SHARING
AND LEARNING . . .

Blogging's virtuous cycle of sharing to learn and learning to share has transformed how I receive information and how I am inspired by information. I credit this virtuous cycle to helping me make sharper, more strategic business decisions and in helping me to become a more consistent marketing mentor to others.

I invite you to join this conversation because the more people share, the more we all will learn.

If you are already blogging, I ask you to blog more often. If you haven't started reading blogs, I ask you to begin by visiting the Tribal Knowledge blog, which can be found at *www.tribalknowledge.biz*.

Together, we can make this virtuous cycle even more virtuous when more of us share to learn and more of us learn to share.

See you on the other side at *www.tribalknowledge.biz*.

NOTES

Tribal Truth 7

1. "Last year [2002], 7.5 cents of every dollar spent in any store in the United States (other than auto-parts stores) went to the retailer." Charles Fishman, "The Wal-Mart You Don't Know," *Fast Company*, December 2003, pg. 73.

2. Ann Zimmerman, "Wal-Mart Sets Out to Prove It's in Vogue," *Wall Street Journal*, August 25, 2005.

3. Hubert Herring, "Wal-Mart's Profits: Nearly $20,000 (Per Minute, That Is)," *New York Times*, February 27, 2005.

Tribal Truth 32

1. Tom Peters, "The Wow Project," *Fast Company*, May 1999, pg. 116.

Tribal Truth 33

1. Gretchen Weber, "Preserving the Starbucks Counter Culture," *Workforce*, February 2005, pg. 34.

Tribal Truth 38

1. BusinessWire, "Starbucks Entertainment and Lions Gate Announce a Partnership That Transforms Traditional Motion Picture Marketing and Distribution Model," forbes.com, January 12, 2006.

Tribal Truth 47

1. Source: National Commission on Entrepreneurship

2. Rhonda Adams, "Focus on Success, Not Failure," *USA Today*, May 6, 2004.

The Starbucks Executive Bookshelf

If there is one commonality between Starbucks executives, it is they all read—a lot. Visit the office of any Starbucks executive and you'll find shelves full of business books.

The following list, in alphabetical order, highlights the most common books virtually all Starbucks executives have read. Each of these listed books have had (and most are still having) a profound impact in shaping how Starbucks does business.

The Art of Innovation, Tom Kelley (Currency Doubleday, 2001)

Be Our Guest, The Disney Institute (Disney Editions, 2001)

Becoming a Category of One, Joe Calloway (Wiley, 2003)

Built for Growth, Arthur Rubinfeld (Wharton Press, 2005)

Built to Last, Jim Collins and Jerry Porras (HarperBusiness, 1997)

Creating Customer Evangelists, Ben McConnell and Jackie Huba (Dearborn, 2002)

The Discipline of Market Leaders, Michael Treacy and Fred Wiersema (Perseus Books, 1995)

Discovering the Soul of Service, Leonard Berry (Free Press, 1999)

18 Immutable Laws of Corporate Reputation, Ronald Alsop (Wall Street Journal Books, 2004)

Emotional Branding, Marc Gobe (Allworth Press, 2001)

First Things First, Stephen Covey (Free Press, 1996)

Good to Great, Jim Collins (HarperBusiness, 2001)

The Imagineering Way, The Imagineers (Disney Editions, 2003)

Love Is the Killer App, Tim Sanders (Crown, 2002)

Lovemarks, Kevin Roberts (PowerHouse Books, 2004)

A New Brand World, Scott Bedbury (Viking, 2002)

Now, Discover Your Strengths, Marcus Buckingham (Free Press, 2001)

Orbiting the Giant Hairball, Gordon MacKenzie (Viking, 1998)

Pour Your Heart into It, Howard Schultz (Hyperion, 1997)

Profit From the Core, Chris Zook (Harvard Business School, 2001)

Purple Cow, Seth Godin (Portfolio, 2003)

Rules of the Red Rubber Ball, Kevin Carroll (ESPN Books, 2005)

Selling The Dream, Guy Kawasaki (HarperBusiness, 1992)

The Servant Leader, James Autry (Three Rivers Press, 2004)

Servant Leadership, Robert Greenleaf (Paulist, 1983)

To Do Doing Done, G. Lynne Snead (Fireside, 1997)

Trading Up, Michael Silverstein and Neil Fiske (Portfolio, 2003)

The Transparent Leader, Herb Baum (HarperBusiness, 2004)

Unstuck, Keith Yamashita and Sandra Spataro (Portfolio, 2004)

Why We Buy, Paco Underhill (Simon & Schuster, 2000)

Wisdom of Teams, Jon Katzenbach and Douglas Smith (HarperBusiness, 2003)

AUTHOR APPRECIATIONS

This book wouldn't be possible without the influences of so many people, places, and things. While I cannot begin to list all the influences in my life, I can (and should) make a go of it. So below is a sampling of a few people, handful of places, and some things that have played a role in shaping me and thus . . . shaping this book.

Hold up. A line listing doesn't do **Lisa Denney Compton** enough justice. *Thank you Lisa for taking a chance and hiring an inexperienced, yet eager-to-learn marketing whippersnapper into the Starbucks tribe. Without you Lisa, this book would not exist.* Nor does simply listing **Paul Williams** do him justice. *Thanks, Paul, for all the marketing fodder and everlasting laughter—we sure did have fun making marketing happen at Starbucks, didn't we?* Lisa and Paul, I am a smarter marketer because of you two.

And because of Alex Lubertozzi and Jennifer Barrell of Prologue Publishing Services, I was able to go from being a blogger to more of a writer. Thank you for your expert assistance in massaging the *Tribal Knowledge* manuscript. Plus the entire crew at Kaplan Business, namely Karen Murphy, Michael Cunningham, Trey Thoelcke, and Leslie Banks, deserve mucho appreciations for having the confidence in me to share the lessons I learned from working inside Starbucks.

With those appreciations out of the way, it's back to our originally scheduled line listing of influential people, places, and things . . .

AC Goodman, Afrika Bambaataa, Aileen Carrell, Alan Hilowitz, Alex Pentland, Alice Meadows, Amy Hopfensperger, Andrew Dillman, Andy Bey, Anna David, Anna Sandilands, Anne Breese, Anthony Carroll, Audrey Lincoff, Barleywines, Bernard Purdie, Bertha Gonzaba, Beth Bilderback, Bill Pearse, Bill Withers, Billie Holiday, Blair Moore, Blastmaster KRS-ONE, Bobby Breve, Bootsy's Rubber Band, Bottleworks, Breakestra, Brian Jackson, Brian Melodia, Bridget Barrett, Brooks Robinson, Bryan Shaw, Cascade hops, Cecile Hudon, Charlie Hunter, Cheri Libby, Chris Gimbl, Chris Gorley, Chris Schultz, Chuck Nevitt, Crane Stavig, Dan Lewis, Dave Olsen, David Brewster, David Garraway, David Smith, Dawn Sandberg-Sviat, Debra Ely, Decade IPA, Dexter Gordon, Dogfish Head Brewing, Don MacKinnon, Don Nose, Dr. Lonnie Smith, Draft House, Duck Island Saloon, Dusty Groove Records, Ed Beazer, Eddie Compton, Elisa Venezia, Elysian Brewing Co., Eric Dolphy, Fela Kuti, Frank the Lion, Fred Wesley, Funkadelic, GABF, Gary Bowsher, Gateway Community Church, Gil Scott-Heron, Ginger Man, Grandmaster Flash, Grandmaster Melle Mel, Grant Green, Grandmixer DST, Green Muse Café,

Greyboy All-Stars, Guru, Gus Dracopouluos, Hannah Moore, Headhunters, Heidi Durham, Heywood McGuffe, Holly Gray, Holly Hinton, Honey Smith Thompson, Hope Broucek, Imperial IPAs, Jackie Moore, Jeff Stollenwerck, Jeff Teabeaux, Jeremy "J-Dawg" Chou, Jerry Thorpe, Jerusalem Tavern, Jessica McCann-Cobb, Jesus Christ, Jim Morgan, Jim Walewander, John Coltrane, John Rheinberger, Jon Greenawalt, Jonathan Seigel, Josh Gibson, Julie Key, Julie Zogg, Karin Koonings, Kate Bovey, Kate Lowery, Keith Stewart, Kelly Krauss, Ken Mooney, Kevan Hayes, Kevin Carothers, Kim Harnish, Kimberly Gerber, Kool Herc, Kurtis Blow, Lakim Shabazz, Lana Moor, Lauren Moore, Lara Stark, Lawrence Trice, Lisa Rauliuk, Lori Carson, Luke Latte, Lynn Eckert, Maceo Parker, Maktub, Margaret Wittenberg, Margie Giuntini, Marla Loftus, Martha Gilkey, Martha Nielsen, Marty Moore, Matt Avalanche, Matt Steele, Megan Olsen, Meters, Michael Duffield, Mike Rogers, Miles Davis, Mr. Friendel, Nancy Kane, Nicky Shaw, Nighthawk, Nona Evans, Onalee Bliley, Parliament, Partners from Starbucks Store #677 ('94 & '95), Paul Curhan, Paul Gabrielson, Pee Wee Ellis, Peggy Iacavoni, Pharaoh Sanders, Pizza Port, Pliny the Elder, Public Enemy, Rebecca Siegmund, Ric Flair, Sammie Barr, Schoolly D, Shannon Donohue, Shannon Jones, Shelagh Hornung, Skerik, Sly Stone, Sonny Rollins, Stacy Elwell-Chalmers, Sue Mecklenburg, Susan Flannery, Suzanne Hall, Tamara Zimmer, Teri Yaki, The Buttamakers, The Von Erichs, Tim Casey, Tim Kern, Too Many Beers, Trevor Boomstra, Trey Shaw, Trip Moore, Two Beers, Valerie Koelzer Johnson, Wendy Beckman, Westvleteren 12, Willie Medina, Wilt Chamberlain, and Yeman Mocha.

A special shout-out to some bloggers, writers, and marketing clairvoyants . . .

Aaron Dignan, Alex Wipperfürth, Al Ries, Andy Morgan, Andy Sernovitz, Anita Sharpe, Ben McConnell, Christopher Locke, Chuck Nyren, Dan Pink, Darren Rovell, Dave Balter, Douglas Rushkoff, David Weinberger, David Wolfe, Doc Searls, Douglas Atkin, DUST!N, Ed Keller, Erik Hansen, Evelyn Rodriguez, Fred Wiersema, Garr Reynolds, Geno Church, George Silverman, Guy Kawasaki, Heath Row, Howard Mann, Hugh MacLeod, Jackie Huba, Jeffrey J. Fox, Jennifer Rice, John Jantsch, John Winsor, Johnnie Moore, Jon Berry, Jon Strande, Karen Post, Katherine Stone, Kathy Sierra, Laura Ries , Lior Arussy, Malcolm Gladwell, Marc Babej, Marc Gobe, Mark Ramsey, Michael Treacey, Mike Landman, Nettie Hartsock, Paco Underhill, Patricia Ryan Madson, Paul Rand, Peter Davidson, Rich…!, Rick Warren, Robbin Phillips, Robert May, Robert Scoble, Robert Spector, Sam Decker, Scott Ginsberg, Sergio Zyman, Seth Godin, Shel Isreal, Spike Jones, Steve Rubel, Tim Manners, Todd Sattersten, Tom Asacker, Tom Peters, and Virginia Miracle.